101 985 035 3

Sheffield Hallam University
Learning and IT Services
Adsetts Centre City Campus
Sheffield S1 1WS

Drama Sessions for Primary Schools and Drama Clubs

Drama Sessions for Primary Schools and Drama Clubs is an indispensable guide designed to help you run effective and enjoyable drama sessions in your primary school for a whole academic year.

The author outlines 33 practical and user-friendly sessions, each one built around developing the social skills needed by children to become effective and positive communicators. Each session has guided time allocations and thorough explanations of what each exercise should achieve. The final session of the term culminates in a 'show and tell' performance in which children can show their family and friends what they have learnt.

As well as the sessions, this book also includes:

- links to the National Curriculum and SEAL;
- notes on 'performance';
- health and safety;
- extra sessions for use in smaller spaces;
- explanations of the pedagogical benefits of every exercise.

This unique and practical book will be of interest to all teachers who need to incorporate drama into everyday classroom learning as well as drama teachers and practitioners looking to run successful, interesting and fun drama sessions for their primary pupils.

Alison Day runs her own drama company, Drama Vision, and has been teaching in primary schools for ten years.

SHEFFIELD HALLAM UNIVERSITY
LEARNING CENTRE
WITHDRAWN FROM STOCK

D1615466

Drama Sessions for Primary Schools and Drama Clubs

Alison Day

Routledge
Taylor & Francis Group

LONDON AND NEW YORK

This first edition published 2011
by Routledge
2 Park Square, Milton Park, Abingdon, Oxon, OX14 4RN

Simultaneously published in the USA and Canada
by Routledge
711 Third Avenue, New York, NY 10017

Routledge is an imprint of the Taylor & Francis Group, an informa business

© 2011 Alison Day

The right of Alison Day to be identified as author of this work has been asserted
by her in accordance with sections 77 and 78 of the Copyright, Designs and
Patents Act 1988.

All rights reserved. No part of this book may be reprinted or reproduced or
utilised in any form or by any electronic, mechanical, or other means, now known
or hereafter invented, including photocopying and recording, or in any
information storage or retrieval system, without permission in writing from the
publishers.

Trademark notice: Product or corporate names may be trademarks or registered
trademarks, and are used only for identification and explanation without intent to
infringe.

British Library Cataloguing in Publication Data
A catalogue record for this book is available from the British Library

Library of Congress Cataloging-in-Publication Data
Day, Alison.
Drama sessions for primary schools and drama clubs / by Alison Day. — 1st ed.
    p. cm.
Includes bibliographical references.
1. Drama—Study and teaching (elementary)—Great Britain. 2. Drama in
education—Great Britain. I. Title.
PN1701.D39 2011
372.66—dc22
2010041386

ISBN13: 978-0-415-60338-6 (pbk)
ISBN13: 978-0-203-82730-7 (ebk)

Typeset in Helvetica
by FiSH Books, Enfield

SHEFFIELD HALLAM UNIVERSITY
WL
TP 792
DA
ADSETTS LEARNING CENTRE

Printed and bound in Great Britain by the MPG Books Group

Contents

This book is dedicated to my very own aspiring actors:
Teddy and Ruby Day.

With special thanks to:
My husband Gary, my supportive parents Alan and Rosemary
and my sister Sharon.

With immense gratitude to:
Lynne Discroll, Phillip Raymond and Jitka Kimonos.

Preface

With extended schools programming it is becoming more challenging for schools to top and tail the school day with varied and innovative clubs that can be rewarding, enriching and full of fun. To my knowledge, primary schools very rarely offer drama clubs to their pupils. In my opinion the main reason for this is because there are no resources readily available to establish and guide the direction of their new club. The teacher's passion for drama alone does not substitute for the lack of available resources and extra time required to locate, read and then decipher the information into a weekly session that grows into a termly structure and then a yearly group. This is why I decided to write this book. I have been an after-school drama club teacher for the past ten years. I established my company Drama Vision with the aim of bringing drama to primary pupils, and the hope of eliminating the self-conscious high-school student who suddenly has drama scheduled in their weekly timetable.

Drama is not about creating the *prima donna*. Yes, it looks at dramatic skills such as voice projection, stage presence and polishing performances, but it is so much more than that. Drama helps children with life skills. It helps to break down social barriers by building personal confidence and self-esteem. It provides children with an outlet to self-express and explore their imaginations through creative play. It develops interpersonal skills through teamwork, role play and social interaction. It allows children to experiment and develop their verbal and non-verbal communication skills.

Drama affects all aspects of daily life, and for children it is a crucial aspect of successful personal development and gaining a feeling of inclusion. Drama is introduced to children through the primary National Curriculum and this book is designed to help support that introduction by utilising selected exercises for the classroom environment (see Chapter 2, Relating to the National Curriculum). However, having a drama club that targets both the extroverts and the introverts means your school is actively providing a very necessary service to society and helping to change behaviours at the grass roots level. Children who are confident naturally have positive dispositions and resilience, and this in turn can make overall classroom work more productive.

So in your hands is all you need to start and guide your drama club; three terms with 11 sessions per term; ten years' worth of practical knowledge and experience with an abundance of fresh ideas developed and created personally by myself and enjoyed – and still being enjoyed – by hundreds of children in drama club.

Go for it – and good luck!

Teacher's notes

This book requires you to do no further preparation for your drama club. It is designed to be a 'pick up and go' style manual for a weekly drama class spanning three terms. Ideally, you should start your new club with term 1 (rather term 2 if starting during the spring term) as the sessions are designed to gradually build up the skills of the members. Be aware that new members will join your drama club at each intake, but this shouldn't derail the overall progressive nature of the work. The core members will embrace the new members and continue to carry the work forward.

Repetition

Remember that children like familiarity to some extent, so you will notice that each session during the first term starts with the name game. This provides the children who lack confidence with instant reassurance, knowing what will be expected from them before the new experience is explored. I have been running drama clubs for over ten years and I still do the name game at the beginning of most sessions due to its popularity.

Success

You may already be familiar with some of the exercises or even witness them daily in the school playground. It is my opinion and experience that the value of these exercises outweighs any view that states that they are 'dated' or past their 'use-by' date. These elected 'golden oldies' provide trusted, rock-solid guarantees of success, and any teacher who is starting out in drama also needs that assurance. Therefore I have carefully collated these into a working format that complements the unison of old and new.

Performances

Everyone has a perception of what drama is and none more so than parents. Everyone will be expecting a performance of sorts, and at first you may think this book doesn't contain one. In fact it contains three performances: one at the end of each term – Parental Sessions. It's not a traditional performance, scripted and rehearsed, but a more developmental approach of involving parents by observing their children at work/play where they can assess their child's personal development from term to term. This innovative approach has proved to be very popular in my experience and parents love to come along with grandparents in tow to watch the 'show and tell' approach and believe it to be just as (if not more) valuable to the cause. So this book is designed to complement and work in coalition with the school's current production programme and hopefully spur on members from the drama club to more demanding roles in curriculum scheduled performances.

Social science

Each game/exercise has detailed instructions on how best to deliver the content in a punchy and child-friendly way. I have also explained in expressive detail in 'The purpose of exercise' the objectives each exercise is aiming to achieve within the social spectrum and personal development of each child. Having the theory of practice enables the teacher to manipulate and direct the work in the proven direction. The highlighted key phrases are designed to provide a quick-glance reference guide to help remind the teacher at an instant.

Timings

Most clubs for this age range is based on a time-frame of approximately one hour. However, once everyone has reached the designated space, refreshed themselves with either a snack and a drink (highly recommended due to the style of work to be endeavoured) and settled down for the register, you really only have a 45-minute session. So these plans are designed around that format. However, if you choose to extend the actual club time to 60 minutes you will find it very easy to extend each exercise by five minutes by just allowing more turns or for the creative play to continue a little longer. The teacher will be the best judge at allocating the time, and at first delivery of the content you will feel pressurised to actually fit it all in!

Space relocation

Experience has proved that on occasion you will find your normal space is unavailable and in order to continue the club programme you will find yourself in a classroom. Therefore, I have provided a selection of three emergency session plans designed specifically for the smaller space. Normal session plans will not adapt to a smaller space and this back-up plan is in place, ready if needed.

Keeping safe within the space

When children are outside their normal boundaries they tend to get a little over-excited. Be sure to assess each space for risks and try to move bags and coats etc. to one side of the space, so tripping up and spilling drinks do not occur where the drama takes place. Be sure to explain to the children that this is a drama club and not a gym club. You will be amazed how many handstands and football dives appear (for example in the name game). Try to influence the children to create and invent more dramatic movements rather than the typical PE-based moves. For reference only, I have included a generic risk assessment form for you to base your assessment on. Schools have their own systems in place, but you can never be too careful with after-school clubs and the extra diligence will pay off.

CHAPTER 2

Relating to the National Curriculum

Drama has a significant part in the primary National Curriculum and I wanted this book to be a direct reference guide for teachers implementing drama within the current literacy framework. I have included a table providing a quick-reference guide to which main exercises relate directly to each year's target objectives. I have also indicated which of those exercises can be utilised in a classroom and which will need the bigger space.

Literacy Framework for Drama: Key Stage 1

Year group	Sessions where Main Exercises relate directly to the											
	1.1	2.1	3.1	4.1	5.1	6.1	7.1	8.1	9.1	10.1	1.2	2.2
Foundation Stage												
Use language to imagine and recreate roles and experiences.					✔★	✔★	✔	✔		✔★	✔★	✔
Year 1												
Explore familiar themes and characters through improvisation and role play.		✔			✔★	✔★	✔	✔	✔★	✔★	✔★	✔
Act out their own and well-known stories using voices for characters.					✔★	✔★			✔★	✔★		✔
Discuss why they like a performance.										✔★		
Year 2												
Adopt appropriate roles in small or large groups and consider alternative courses of action.				✔		✔★				✔★		
Present parts of traditional stories, their own stories or work drawn from different parts of the curriculum for members of their own class.						✔★				✔★		
Consider how mood and atmosphere are created in live or recorded performance.				✔			✔	✔		✔★		

★ = can be classroom-based

National Curriculum standards within the Literacy Framework

3.2	4.2	5.2	6.2	7.2	8.2	9.2	10.2	1.3	2.3	3.3	4.3	5.3	6.3	7.3	8.3	9.3	10.3
	✔★	✔		✔	✔★	✔★	✔★			✔★	✔★	✔	✔	✔	✔	✔	✔
✔		✔	✔	✔	✔★	✔★	✔★			✔★		✔	✔	✔	✔	✔	✔
	✔★	✔	✔	✔	✔★	✔★	✔★			✔★	✔★	✔	✔	✔	✔	✔	✔
	✔★	✔	✔	✔	✔★	✔★	✔★					✔	✔	✔	✔	✔	✔
		✔	✔														
	✔★				✔★	✔★	✔★			✔★	✔★						

Literacy Framework for Drama: Key Stage 2

Year group	Sessions where Main Exercises relate directly to the												
	1.1	2.1	3.1	4.1	5.1	6.1	7.1	8.1	9.1	10.1	1.2	2.2	
Year 3													
Present events and characters through dialogue to engage the interest of an audience.		✔			✔ ★	✔ ★			✔ ★	✔ ★		✔	
Use some drama strategies to explore stories or issues.								✔			✔ ★	✔	
Identify and discuss qualities of others' performances, including gesture, action and costume.	✔		✔ ★			✔ ★		✔	✔ ★		✔ ★		
Year 4													
Create roles showing how behaviour can be interpreted from different viewpoints.					✔ ★			✔			✔ ★		
Develop scripts based on improvisation.													
Comment constructively on plays and performances, discussing effects and how they are achieved.	✔			✔			✔	✔			✔ ★		

★ = can be classroom-based

National Curriculum standards within the Literacy Framework

3.2	4.2	5.2	6.2	7.2	8.2	9.2	10.2	1.3	2.3	3.3	4.3	5.3	6.3	7.3	8.3	9.3	10.3
	✔★	✔	✔	✔	✔★	✔★	✔★			✔★	✔★						
	✔★	✔			✔★	✔★	✔★			✔★	✔★	✔	✔	✔	✔	✔	✔
								✔									
										✔★							
	✔★																
								✔									

Literacy Framework for Drama: Key Stage 2 – continued

Year group	Sessions where Main Exercises relate directly to the												
	1.1	2.1	3.1	4.1	5.1	6.1	7.1	8.1	9.1	10.1	1.2	2.2	
Year 5													
Reflect on how working in role helps to explore complex issues.			✔ ★		✔ ★	✔ ★		✔	✔ ★	✔ ★	✔ ★		
Perform a scripted scene making use of dramatic conventions.													
Use and recognise the impact of theatrical effects in drama.			✔ ★	✔							✔ ★	✔	
Year 6													
Improvise using a range of drama strategies and conventions to explore themes such as hopes, fears and desires.						✔ ★		✔		✔ ★			
Devise a performance considering how to adapt the performance for a specific audience.				✔			✔						
Consider the overall impact of a live or recorded performance, identifying dramatic ways of conveying characters' ideas and building tension.	✔		✔ ★	✔						✔ ★			

★ = can be classroom-based

National Curriculum standards within the Literacy Framework

3.2	4.2	5.2	6.2	7.2	8.2	9.2	10.2	1.3	2.3	3.3	4.3	5.3	6.3	7.3	8.3	9.3	10.3
		✔	✔	✔	✔★	✔★	✔★			✔★	✔★						
	✔★																
✔					✔★	✔★	✔★		✔				✔	✔	✔	✔	✔
											✔★						
										✔★							
								✔	✔		✔★						

Relating to the National Strategies Social and Emotional Aspects of Learning (SEAL)

All seven themes within the SEAL programming lend themselves to exploration through drama. With the aim of helping children develop knowledge, understanding and skills in several key social and emotional aspects of learning, drama can be utilised to explore self-awareness, managing feelings, motivation, empathy and social skills.

I have collated a quick-reference guide that indicates which main exercises relate directly to each theme. Using this chart you can incorporate a dramatic, active and challenging supplement to accompany existing resources. I have also indicated which of these exercises can be utilised in a classroom and those that require a larger space.

Social and Emotional Aspects of Learning (SEAL)

	Sessions where Main Exercises relate directly to												
	1.1	2.1	3.1	4.1	5.1	6.1	7.1	8.1	9.1	10.1	1.2	2.2	
Theme 1: New beginnings													
Offering the children the opportunity to explore feelings of happiness, excitement, sadness, anxiety and fearfulness and to value themselves as individuals.											✔ ★		
Theme 2: Getting on and falling out													
Showing how to value diversity and co-operation through managing feelings, developing social skills of friendship and working well together in group situations.								✔			✔ ★		
Theme 3: Say no to bullying													
Focus on bullying: what it is, how it feels, why people bully, how we can prevent and respond to it through understanding and developing self-awareness, empathy and managing feelings.													

★ = can be conducted in a classroom

	3.2	4.2	5.2	6.2	7.2	8.2	9.2	10.2	1.3	2.3	3.3	4.3	5.3	6.3	7.3	8.3	9.3	10.3
			✔									✔ ★						
								✔			✔ ★							

Social and Emotional Aspects of Learning (SEAL) – continued

	Sessions where Main Exercises relate directly to											
	1.1	2.1	3.1	4.1	5.1	6.1	7.1	8.1	9.1	10.1	1.2	2.2
Theme 4: **Going for goals!**												
Exploring motivation and self-awareness. Having the belief that what you do makes a difference. Introducing self-value.	✔									✔ ★		✔
Theme 5: **Good to be me**												
Focusing on understanding our feelings, self-awareness and managing our personal reactions.							✔				✔ ★	
Theme 6: **Relationships**												
To explore feelings within the context of our important relationships and understand the feelings associated with loss.												
Theme 7: **Changes**												
Exploring children's understanding of different types of change, positive and negative, and common human responses to it.						✔						

★ = can be conducted in a classroom

the National Strategies SEAL programming																	
3.2	4.2	5.2	6.2	7.2	8.2	9.2	10.2	1.3	2.3	3.3	4.3	5.3	6.3	7.3	8.3	9.3	10.3

In the grid, in the column headed **4.3**, the following marks appear:

✔
★

CHAPTER 4

Your drama club: three terms of 11 session plans per term

Club term 1

Warm Up: **Name Game**   **5 mins**

Instructions: With the group standing in a circle facing one another, each member takes a turn to introduce themselves with a movement/action to their name, then the rest of the group copy the action exactly. Example: Alison does a star jump and shouts her name at the same time. The group then copies.

*(Purpose of game: This game allows the child to express themselves as an individual. It looks at **multi-task collaboration**; to move; to speak; to think; all at the same time. This game quickly displays those **with little confidence** and those who will need extra encouragement.)*

Game 1: **Paint Pot Game**   **10 mins**

Instructions: With the group in a circle the teacher takes the lead and the children follow the mime of: taking a paint pot, brush, stick off the top shelf and putting it on the floor between their feet. Opening the paint pot lid with the stick, stirring the paint – ask the children the colour of their paint. Dipping their brush in the paint they choose a place to paint within the room. Bring them back to the circle, explain they are 'bored' with using the paint brush and throw it away over their shoulder. Now they are to use their hands. Ask them to dip their hands in the imaginary paint and put hand prints around the room. Bring them back into the circle, ask them to wipe their hands over their tops to clean them and now use your feet. Bring back to the circle and describe what you see. Example: Red hand prints over the walls, blue foot prints over the floor etc. Then ask them to line up and give each member an imaginary bucket and sponge to clear up their mess. Return to circle on completion.

*(Purpose of game: This game asks the children to follow direction through **listening skills** and improvisation. To use mime to **develop fine motor skills** and help create **individual expression** through group play.)*

Exercise 1: **Mirroring Partners**   **15 mins**

Instructions: Ask the group to team up into pairs of similar height. The children then decide who is A and who is B. Facing one another A copies the moves B makes as if they are looking into a mirror. Small moves are to be encouraged so the copying can be precise. Example: B scratches head and A copies movement exactly. Develop to strong movements such as balancing and synchronised movements. Example: Balancing on left leg whilst touching nose with right hand. Swap leaders so B copies A movements. Then try having no leader and use involuntary movements to start the copying process. Example: A looking at B, A fidgets with skirt involuntarily, B copies the fidget movement and, in turn, A copies B and movement sequence has started.

*(Purpose of exercise: By working in pairs this exercise explores **leadership qualities as well as negotiation skills**. The children will be either encouraged to take the leadership role when usually they prefer not to, or to take a secondary role when they would often volunteer to be the leader. Movement and co-ordination is experimented with through the observation process. This in turn will help to develop the brain's cognitive process through **relaying exact information from sight to movement succinctly** and will further the development of fine motor skills.)*

Exercise 2: **Sculptors** **15 mins**

Instructions: Ask the group to find different pairs and choose between the roles of sculptor and clay. The sculptor is then allotted time to create the clay (person) into a statue by moulding and placing the body into positions. Encourage the sculptor to have precise positioning and attention to detail and ask the clay to retain the position in a frozen state. Example: Sculptor makes a roaring lion from the clay by placing their partner on their hands and knees with mouth open. Then ask all sculptors to gather round and, in turn, visit each clay model, try guessing what the statue is and discussing how the positioning of the person (clay) helped convey that impression. You can ask the model to come to life to add further role play. Swap roles within partners and repeat the exercise.

*(Purpose of exercise: Looks at **developing individual work** through **expression, concentration and focus**. It also looks at giving and **receiving praise for individual effort**.)*

Total time: 45 mins

Warm Up: **Name Game** **5 mins**

Instructions: With the group in a circle facing one another, each member takes a turn to introduce themselves with a movement/action to their name, then the rest of the group copy the action exactly. Example: Alison does a star jump and shouts her name at the same time. The group then copies.

*(Purpose of game: This game allows the child to express themselves as an individual. It looks at **multi-task collaboration**; to move; to speak; to think; all at the same time. This game quickly displays those **with little confidence** and those who will need extra encouragement.)*

Game 1: **Bake a Cake** **10 mins**

Instructions: Standing in a circle, ask the children to follow your mime of: reaching up and opening a cupboard, getting out the flour and sugar packets, and placing them on the imaginary table in front of them. Bend down and open the imaginary fridge, reach for the eggs, milk and butter and place them on the table top. From the imaginary cupboard behind you, get out the mixing bowl and cake tin and place them on top of the table. From the side drawer, get out the spoon and butter knife. Direct the children to mime the following: placing flour and sugar into a bowl – mix; breaking the egg, pouring the milk and slicing some butter into the mixing bowl – mix. Ask who can mix the fastest. Ask children to find a special ingredient they would like to add to the mixture. Example: chocolate chips, cherries – mix. Place the mixture into the cake tin then lick the spoon. Say 'yum'. Put on imaginary oven gloves, turn round and set the imaginary timer and oven heat by turning knobs. Place cake tin into the oven. Cross your arms and whistle for time to pass. Sniff the air and ask the children if they can smell their cake cooking? Call out 'ding' to represent the timer; with gloves still on, turn off oven, take cake out, blow cake to cool. Place cake on plate and cut a slice to eat. Mime eating cake. Ask children to place the remaining cake by their coats so they remember to take it home at the end of the session. End sitting in circle.

*(Purpose of game: The children are asked to follow direction and **improve their attention to detail and focusing skills**. It helps to improve listening skills and **working as an individual within a group setting**. It also complements fine motor skill development.)*

Exercise 1: **Animal Kingdom** **15 mins**

Instructions: Select one male and one female member of the group to be the King and Queen of the Animal Kingdom. Set two chairs (thrones) for them on one side of the room. The rest of the class are to sit opposite the chairs waiting

Drama Sessions for Primary Schools and Drama Clubs

for the King and Queen to enter with royal-like actions and sit upon the thrones. Example: Queen to wave hand in the air whilst King marches in. Once seated the King and Queen decide upon an animal of their choice to come and visit them. They do this by calling out to the rest of the group: 'COME TO ME MY...lions. ...' The rest of the group are then to travel through the space doing their best impression of that animal. Example: Crawling on hands and knees whilst roaring. Once they have reached the King and Queen they sit and cower down, still acting as that animal. The King and Queen feed the animals and the group continues to act the animal's feeding habits. Example: Tearing meat to shreds and gobbling it down. Then everyone relaxes and the King and Queen choose the best boy and girl animal performance and the chosen ones take the new place of royalty. Repeat.

*(Purpose of exercise: This exercise starts to explore **physical development**. It explores changing posture and positioning of the body to represent something else. Starts to create spacial, physical awareness and **interpersonal skills** such as proximity values.)*

Exercise 2: **Toy Box** **15 mins**

Instructions: With the group standing in a circle, choose a boy and girl to curl up into small balls inside the circle. The rest of the group sing whilst waving their arms up and down. 'Toys from the toy box come and see, Toys from the toy box play with me.' The two chosen pupils jump up (as if like a Jack-in-the-box) from inside the circle and announce which toy they are. Example: rag doll, robot. The circle then breaks for the two toys to come out and walk around the room in their chosen style. Example: rag doll – all floppy; robot – stiff, quick movements. The rest of the group are to choose which one to copy and all then perform. Repeat.

*(Purpose of exercise: This exercise channels positive behaviour and self-expression. It helps to **create self-worth and confidence** as it allows instant praise for notable efforts. It encourages the children to make **independent decisions under pressure** and within time constraints.)*

Total time: 45 mins

Drama Sessions for Primary Schools and Drama Clubs

Warm Up: **Name Game**   **5 mins**

Instructions: With the group in a circle facing one another, each member takes a turn to introduce themselves with a movement/action to their name, then the rest of the group copy the action exactly. Example: Alison does a star jump and shouts her name at the same time. The group then copies.

*(Purpose of game: This game allows the child to express themselves as an individual. It looks at **multi-task collaboration**; to move; to speak; to think; all at the same time. This game quickly displays those **with little confidence** and those who will need extra encouragement.)*

Game 1: **The Plasticine Pass**   **10 mins**

Instructions: With the group sitting in a circle, take an imaginary lump of plasticine and roll it into an object of use. Example: toothbrush, hairbrush. Perform a mime action so members can guess the object. Then pass the object to the person to the right, who uses it for a short time and then squashes the object to make their new object. Continue around the circle until the end.

*(Purpose of game: This simple game starts to build improvisation skills with **independent thinking and expression**. It allows you to give **one-to-one encouragement** to every pupil in a focused setting. It allows personal praise and acknowledgement, and this in turn builds confidence.)*

Exercise 1: **Animal Crackers**   **15 mins**

Instructions: Ask the group to find an individual space within the room. Working independently, they are to grow from a small ball shape on the floor into the chosen animal during a count of 5. Example: The chosen animal is a giraffe and from a small ball they slowly grow into a tall long shape whilst the teacher counts to 5. On 5, they can make the animal noise but they are not to move about the space. Make sure it is a progression and not a hurried trans-formation. Ask one member to run amongst the statues and choose the best impression and repeat.

*(Purpose of exercise: This exercise is all about **self-control**. It introduces timing and patience with a gradual build-up to an end result. It is about **creating a journey** through building blocks and not just about a beginning or an end-product. This in turn helps to create control of both feelings and emotions through dramatic play.)*

Exercise 2: **Clap to It**　　　　　　　　　　　　　　　　　**15 mins**

Instructions: Ask the group to gather in one corner of the room. Select one member to leave the room and another to choose a designated area within the room. Example: The door handle, the fire extinguisher, the light switch. Ask the excluded member to return to the room and explore the space by walking and touching things whilst the group clap quietly, if the person is not close/near to the spot, and loudly if near to it. Discuss how well the members are interpreting the clapping sounds and how it feels to react and provide sound signals. Repeat.

*(Purpose of exercise: This exercise introduces **non-verbal communication skills and teambuilding**. Using unusual forms of communication (volume of clapping) allows the children to explore and experiment with **messaging of sound**. It challenges the lone child to **interpret the form of communication** into an action without direct instructions. This exercise helps to introduce the social skill of reading/interpreting non-verbal communication skills and making autonomous conclusions without being told directly. It also looks at group work and team management in order to create a cohesive result.)*

Total time: 45 mins

Warm Up: **Name Game**   **5 mins**

Instructions: With the group in a circle facing one another, each member takes a turn to introduce themselves with a movement/action to their name, then the rest of the group copy the action exactly. Example: Alison does a star jump and shouts her name at the same time. The group then copies.

(Purpose of game: This game allows the child to express themselves as an individual. It looks at **multi-task collaboration***; to move; to speak; to think; all at the same time. This game quickly displays those* **with little confidence** *and those who will need extra encouragement.)*

Game 1: **Talking Gibberish**   **10 mins**

Instructions: Standing in a circle, start by asking a pair to talk to each other in an alien language. They are to talk in conversation, answering back and forth in a language of noises. Example: Making whistle-like noises, one person asks for directions to the local library. The second person replies in popping sounds that they do not know. You are allowed to use physical contributions. Example: Waving, pointing as well as facial expressions to help convey the question. It is important that the conversation still happens even if they are not sure what their partner is talking about, as this is part of the fun. Work around the circle until every member has had a turn.

(Purpose of game: This game is all about **breaking inhibitions and building confidence***. Being silly is often fun, and this exercise allows the children to release their fears of feeling and looking silly in front of others. If we are all made to look silly we can all laugh at one another. Then we can start to* **build self-confidence** *by understanding that the normal feeling of uncertainty is just part of an emotional journey, and not something that should stop us from enjoying a new experience.)*

Exercise 1: **Save Me**   **15 mins**

Instructions: With everyone standing in a circle place a chair in the middle. In complete silence and using eye contact alone the teacher (walking member) starts the game by slowly walking towards a chosen member (the target) and touching the chair *en route*. The target must be saved and they can do this by requesting help from another member within the circle (the saviour). They do this by saying *Target: 'Save me . . . Richard . . . '.* The response by the *saviour* should be: *'Come here . . . Samantha . . . '.* The target is then saved and starts to walk across the circle (touching the chair *en route*) towards their saviour, whilst the original walking member stands in the vacant circle space. Now the saviour becomes the new target and has to be saved by calling out for help from another member in the circle – a new saviour. If, however, the target is not saved in time and the walking person reaches the target before they have been saved, the target is out of the game and sits on the floor and the walking person stands next to them in the circle. The teacher then continues the game by walking towards a new target as above.

*(Purpose of exercise: This exercise requires complete **focus and concentration**. The rules encourage forethought and **independent problem-solving** within a short time limit. This exercise allows the child to acknowledge and then process visual information, which then requires a rapid response. Example: Who is walking to me? Why are they walking towards me? What do I need to do now?)*

Exercise 2: **Mime in a Box**   **15 mins**

Instructions: Ask everyone to find an isolated spot in the space facing you. Lead the group through a simple mime (no words) of opening a large cardboard box, stepping into the box and closing the box lid on top of themselves. Jump out of the box like a jack-in-the-box and then step out of the box. Then continue to lead the mime by finding a solid door locked in front of you. Try to push the door open, try to pull the door open. Look around the immediate space for the key to open the locked door. Find the key in your pocket, put the key into the lock, unlock the door, push open the door and step through, close and lock the door behind you. Continue the mime by making a cup of tea. Pour the tea, pour the milk and put two sugar lumps into the tea and stir. Mime sitting and drinking your tea. Discuss how it feels to not use your voice and how that can manipulate and accentuate movement.

*(Purpose of exercise: This exercise is all about allowing the **imagination to lead the physical action**. In its simple context it helps to build **creative expression** with precise attention to detail. It also helps with **personal awareness** and the way the body moves.)*

Total time: 45 mins

Warm Up: **Name Game** **5 mins**

Instructions: With the group in a circle facing one another, each member takes a turn to introduce themselves with a movement/action to their name, then the rest of the group copy the action exactly. Example: Alison does a star jump and shouts her name at the same time. The group then copies.

*(Purpose of game: This game allows the child to express themselves as an individual. It looks at **multi-task collaboration**; to move; to speak; to think; all at the same time. This game quickly displays those with **little confidence** and those who will need extra encouragement.)*

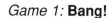

Game 1: **Bang!** **15 mins**

Instructions: Standing in a circle explain you are all cowboys and cowgirls with two pistols in your holsters. The teacher starts the game by calling a member's name. That person then ducks to the floor and the two people either side have a shoot-out by pointing their fingers at each other and shouting 'bang'. The first person to say the word bang is the winner, and the loser sits down in their circle placement. If, however, the person whose name is called does not duck down quickly enough, they are out, as they get hit by the bullets from the shoot-out. When only two people are left standing they step into the middle of the circle and place themselves back-to-back as if in a 'showdown'. They step three steps away from each other and listen for a selected member of the sitting crowd to shout the word bang, on which they turn and shoot each other by shouting the word bang. The ultimate winner is the person who shouts 'bang' first.

*(Purpose of game: This game is all about **focus**. The group has to remain focused throughout the whole exercise in order to prevent losing. The game changes each time a player sits out, so it is about **processing the ever-changing information correctly** and adapting your actions accordingly. It also allows self-expression, as it produces an authorised emotional outlet in a controlled context.)*

Exercise 1: **Hot-Seating** **25 mins**

Instructions: Place a chair in front of the group who are sitting on the floor in an audience position. Explain that the group are journalists about to meet a person to whom they are to ask questions and guess what job they do. The rules are that the chosen person can only answer the questions with a yes or no. Choose a member to come and select a piece of paper (tabs) from your envelope. The piece of paper will have a job description which the chosen person is to act and answer the questions about. Encourage probing questions. Example: Do you wear a uniform? rather than: Is your hair black?

Drama Sessions for Primary Schools and Drama Clubs

police	firefighter	astronaut	farmer	ballet dancer
king/queen	dentist	doctor	scientist	vet

*(Purpose of exercise: This exercise introduces **role play** and helps to develop creative thought. It also builds self-control as it has a format/rules to adhere to. It **introduces the skill of improvisation** (making it up on the spot with no rehearsal or pre-planning) in its simplest form.)*

Total time: 45 mins

Warm Up: **Name Game**   **5 mins**

Instructions: With the group in a circle facing one another, each member takes a turn to introduce themselves with a movement/action to their name, then the rest of the group copy the action exactly. Example: Alison does a star jump and shouts her name at the same time. The group then copies.

(Purpose of game: This game allows the child to express themselves as an individual. It looks at **multi-task collaboration***; to move; to speak; to think; all at the same time. This game quickly displays those with* **little confidence** *and those who will need extra encouragement.)*

Game 1: **Duck, Duck, Goose**   **5 mins**

Instructions: Sitting in a circle one member is chosen to walk around the circle tapping the sitting members' heads and saying the word 'duck' as they pass. On their choice, they tap someone's head and say 'Goose', and that person then stands up. The two members then race around the circle and the first one back to the vacant position is the winner and sits down in that spot. The loser then starts the game again by tapping heads and saying the word 'duck'.

(Purpose of game: This game helps to create **team bonding and union***. It allows the children to let off steam through championing their fellow members. It channels* **volume control** *as at one given moment everyone can be shouting, and in the next, everyone has to be silent again to hear effectively.)*

Exercise 1: **The Bomb Shelter**    **15 mins**

Instructions: Select five members to stand in front of the group and ask them to each think of a famous person they can impersonate. Explain that they are in World War II and they have all been placed in a bomb shelter for their safety. However, there is only enough equipment and food to help save four lives and one of them will have to leave and fend for themselves in the war zone alone. Each member is to devise a short speech on why they should be allowed to stay and how crucial it is that they survive. Example: The Queen; if she were to die, who would make the decisions that governed the Kingdom? Once everyone has spoken, the group decides who should stay and who should be evicted by clapping. The one with the loudest clapping should be the one that leaves. They act a mini mime of opening the bomb shelter door and evicting them into the war zone. Repeat.

(Purpose of exercise: This exercise is all about **learning negotiation skills***. It looks at how to build a constructive argument and* **how to put across a definitive point of view***. It is all about verbal communication and how to learn to*

Drama Sessions for Primary Schools and Drama Clubs

express their ideas and opinions in a constructive manner. The acting is just the fun tool that allows this exercise to exist.)

Exercise 2: **Famous Pairs** **20 mins**

Instructions: Ask the group to get themselves into pairs and to think of a famous couple. Example: Tom and Jerry, Mickey and Minnie Mouse, Postman Pat and Jess the Cat. Then ask them to devise a short (20 seconds) movement/play to complement their chosen couple. Example: Tom and Jerry might chase after one another with cat and mouse-like movement. Ask the group to sit down as if an audience and take it in turns to show each pairing. The audience is to guess by the action who they are.

*(Purpose of exercise: This introduces **time-frame tasks**. The group is set a small amount of time to **create an end-product to performance quality standard**. It builds independent thinking and problem-solving through creative play. It helps to build **self-confidence** through performance role play and allows direct praise by performing to others.)*

Total time: 45 mins

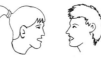

Warm Up: **Name Game** **5 mins**

Instructions: With the group in a circle facing one another, each member takes a turn to introduce themselves with a movement/action to their name, then the rest of the group copy the action exactly. Example: Alison does a star jump and shouts her name at the same time. The group then copies.

*(Purpose of game: This game allows the child to express themselves as an individual. It looks at **multi-task collaboration**; to move; to speak; to think; all at the same time. This game quickly displays those with **little confidence** and those who will need extra encouragement.)*

Game 1: **Gears** **10 mins**

Instructions: Show by example that everyone is to move around the space in four different styles. Gear 1: in a lazy, lethargic slow style. Gear 2: speed walking. Gear 3: jogging in the park listening to their MP3 players. Gear 4: running as fast as they can without bumping into anything or anyone. The teacher is to select different members to stand in the middle of the space who will then randomly call out the numbers. The group is to respond quickly and interchange between the speeds.

*(Purpose of game: This exercise continues to develop cognitive reflexes and looks at **how fast the individual can process verbal information and translate it into a physical action**. It also allows the group to **burn up excess energy** ready to concentrate and focus on the tasks ahead.)*

Exercise 1: **The Elements** **15 mins**

Instructions: Ask each member to find a space within the room. Ask the group to name the different weather elements. Example: snow, rain, sun, wind etc. Then ask a member to show the group how they feel a dramatisation of that weather element might look. Example: snow – a twirling light dance movement; rain – a stomping and pounding of the feet; sun – a lazy slow, exhausting style movement; wind – an arm flapping, leg waggling-swaying style movement. Once the individual has shown their idea, ask the group to devise their personal version and act out around the room as a whole group. Repeat with each weather element.

*(Purpose of exercise: This exercise aids the continued development of physical awareness, but more importantly, it helps to build **creative expression**. Stretching the imagination into a physical form helps them to appreciate and **value their ideas**. With encouragement and **praise, this nurtured confidence** will then encourage them to be more forthcoming in all aspects of expression.)*

Drama Sessions for Primary Schools and Drama Clubs

Exercise 2: **Elements of Performance**   **15 mins**

Instructions: Ask the group to find a new individual space within the room. Discuss what you do and how you behave depending on the type of weather it is outside. Example: snow – become competitive with a snowball fight; rain – rushing everywhere under umbrellas with no time for anyone; sun – relaxed and happy to play outside; wind – frustrated when fighting against the wind. Lead a group improvisation (play) by moving about the space exploring all of the group's ideas one element and idea at a time. To further this exercise, try splitting the class into two smaller groups where one performs and the other observes how the style of movement changes if different performing spaces are experienced. Example: Place the action into an audience theatrical 'round' (the audience encircle the action), 'proscenium' (the audience sit directly in front of the action) or 'arena' (the audience are in tiered heights and levels observing the action).

(Purpose of exercise: This exercise is all about **self-analysis**. *On a very simple level it looks at how the individual behaves under a set of circumstances. On a much deeper level it allows the* **individual to analyse positive and negative behaviours**. *It creates a self-study on how one responds to certain triggers and helps to* **build self-awareness**.*)*

Total time: 45 mins

Warm Up: **Name Game** 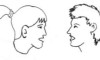   **5 mins**

Instructions: With the group in a circle facing one another, each member takes a turn to introduce themselves with a movement/action to their name, then the rest of the group copy the action exactly. Example: Alison does a star jump and shouts her name at the same time. The group then copies.

*(Purpose of game: This game allows the child to express themselves as an individual. It looks at **multi-task collaboration**; to move; to speak; to think; all at the same time. This game quickly displays those with **little confidence** and those who will need extra encouragement.)*

Game 1: **Pip, Squeak, Alfred**   **10 mins**

Instructions: Sitting in a circle the teacher gives each member a name of either Pip, Squeak or Alfred. The teacher is then to stand in the middle of the circle and call out one of the three names. The members with that name are to get up and race around the circle until the teacher calls out 'home'. Then all running members are to return to their seated positions as fast as possible but without turning around or cutting through the centre of the circle. The last member to sit is out. You can do this game in degrees by calling out more than one name at a time and asking the members to add movements and sounds as they run.

*(Purpose of game: This game helps to build **self-control and teamwork**. Those running have a set of rules to abide by and a challenge to stay in the game by thinking fast and moving faster. The commonality of being cheered helps to build confidence within a competitive structure. It also **introduces the skill of losing**, something that needs to be learnt through nurtured experiences.)*

Exercise 1: **Emotional Statues**   **30 mins**

Instructions: First discuss what an emotion is and the different types we experience. Example: angry, happy, sad etc. Then put the group into smaller groups of either four or five members (see Glossary, Smaller-sized groups). Ask each individual group to create a physical dramatisation of a given emotion with the one rule that everyone must be connected to someone else. The groups are then to prepare a statue of what they believe an emotion could physically look like. Example: angry – each member of the group could place their limbs entwined with each other to represent the feeling of a knotted tangle about to snap under pressure; happy – the idea of floating can be dramatised by holding hands and all leaning slightly backwards and balancing in a state of contentment; sad – create a small ball of everyone hiding behind one another

Drama Sessions for Primary Schools and Drama Clubs

and creating a barrier where no one can see their faces. This can be explored further with more complex emotions such as jealousy, excitement, frustration etc. or by adding slight movement or sounds to the statue. Once the groups have devised their piece, sit the whole group into an audience position and ask them, one by one, to show. After each display discuss why we might feel that way and how we can control that feeling in our everyday lives.

*(Purpose of exercise: This exercise helps to build self-awareness **by translating emotional experiences** into a tangible form. The dramatisation of emotions can help them to **analyse and appreciate feelings** they experience personally. By creating an understanding they can help themselves to break or adapt a pattern of behaviour and build towards **positive social skills**.)*

Total time: 45 mins

 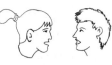

Warm Up: **Name Game** **5 mins**

Instructions: With the group in a circle facing one another, each member takes a turn to introduce themselves with a movement/action to their name, then the rest of the group copy the action exactly. Example: Alison does a star jump and shouts her name at the same time. The group then copies.

*(Purpose of game: This game allows the child to express themselves as an individual. It looks at **multi-task collaboration**; to move; to speak; to think; all at the same time. This game quickly displays those with **little confidence** and those who will need extra encouragement.)*

Game 1: **Swim, Little Fishy, Swim!** **10 mins**

Instructions: Ask the whole group to line up at one end of the room. Explain that the group is all little fishes living and feeding in the coral reef. They are only to make the sounds of popping (to imitate feeding) and to place palm to palm (to imitate swimming). Sadly, one day the food in the coral reef runs out and they have to run to the other side of the space to a new coral reef to feed. However, when crossing the room, they are swimming through shark-infested waters. The shark is one chosen member who starts the swimming by shouting 'Swim, little fishy, swim'. Once the fish are swimming across the space, the shark is to tag as many fish before they become safe on the other side. Once the fish have been tagged, they become seaweed and, rooted to the floor (sitting down), they help the shark to catch the remaining fish. They do this by waving their arms and tagging those swimming close by who then become seaweed too. Eventually, only a few fish swimming across the waters have survived and the winner is the last fish alive.

*(Purpose of game: This game helps to burn up excess energy and helps to build a **team spirit** within the group. Encouraging each other through game play helps to build confidence and **appreciation of one another**.)*

Exercise 1: **999 – Emergency!** **30 mins**

Instructions: Ask the group to sit in an audience position and choose five members to join you in the performance area. Select one member to pull out a tab from your envelope (see below). The selected members are to be cast from the chosen tab and then the teacher is to instruct and direct a mini play/performance in front of the group (improvisation). Be sure to encourage every member to speak out loud. Once the play has finished, the audience members are to guess what emergency service the play related to.

Drama Sessions for Primary Schools and Drama Clubs

Firefighters	Police	Hospital	Coast guard	Breakdown rescue
Member 1: Cat	Member 1: Burglar	Member 1: Person	Member 1: Swimmer	Member 1: Driver
Member 2: Person	Member 2: Person	Member 2: Person	Member 2: Swimmer	Member 2: Passenger
Member 3: Firefighter	Member 3: Police	Member 3: Doctor	Member 3: Call operator	Member 3: Call operator
Member 4: Firefighter	Member 4: Police	Member 4: Nurse	Member 4: Coast guard	Member 4: Mechanic
Member 5: Engine driver	Member 5: Witness	Member 5: Ambulance driver	Member 5: Helicopter pilot	Member 5: Tow truck driver

*(Purpose of exercise: This is the first introduction to devising and creating a performance. Following the direction of the teacher allows each member the support they may need to **feel confident to act out in front of others**. The simple structure allows each member to foresee what might happen without any pre-planning or rehearsal. This in turn encourages the **members to be a little more expressive** rather than apprehensive and inert.)*

Total time: 45 mins

Warm Up: **Name Game** **5 mins**

Instructions: With the group in a circle facing one another, each member takes a turn to introduce themselves with a movement/action to their name, then the rest of the group copy the action exactly. Example: Alison does a star jump and shouts her name at the same time. The group then copies.

(Purpose of game: This game allows the child to express themselves as an individual. It looks at **multi-task collaboration***; to move; to speak; to think; all at the same time. This game quickly displays those* **with little confidence** *and those who will need extra encouragement.)*

Game 1: **Who's Missing?** **10 mins**

Instructions: Ask everyone to move around the space and then the teacher shouts 'freeze', and everyone is to stop still. Then each member is to crawl up to into a small ball and close their eyes. The teacher then indicates to a member by tapping them on the back to quietly exit the space. The teacher then shouts 'move' and everyone is to move around the space again. The teacher then shouts 'freeze' again and the group are to look around and name the missing person. Repeat.

(Purpose of game: This game develops **sensory skills** *and explores a simple form of* **problem-solving***. Being made aware of subtle changes within their environment promotes* **independent thinking** *by analysing a pattern of change and making* **constructive conclusions***.)*

Exercise 1: **Play Acting** **30 mins**

Instructions: Ask the group to sit in an audience position and select five members to join the teacher in the performance area. Ask a selected member to pick out a tab from the envelope (see below) and from the list, cast the mini play (improvisation). Teacher is to direct the simple action by simple question-and-answer scenario. Example tab: park – teacher asks the dog walker what might happen? The member suggests the dog escapes its lead and they have to chase it. Teacher then asks the toddler what could happen? The member suggests they bump their head on the swing etc. Once everyone has suggested their idea the play begins with each member playing out their chosen idea at the same time, making a simple play for the audience members to watch. Don't worry if the ideas aren't cohesive; it is the individual input that matters.

Drama Sessions for Primary Schools and Drama Clubs

Park	Supermarket	Library	Swimming pool	Zoo
Member 1: Dog walker	Member 1: Shopper	Member 1: Young person	Member 1: Swimmer	Member 1: Monkey
Member 2: Dog	Member 2: Till operator	Member 2: Young person	Member 2: Swimmer	Member 2: Lion
Member 3: Toddler	Member 3: Shelf stacker	Member 3: Elderly person	Member 3: Life guard	Member 3: Elephant
Member 4: Mother	Member 4: Boss	Member 4: Librarian	Member 4: Life guard	Member 4: Giraffe
Member 5: Jogger	Member 5: Thief	Member 5: Librarian	Member 5: Receptionist	Member 5: Zoo keeper

*(Purpose of exercise: The main point of this exercise is to introduce **leadership skills** in a very subtle way. Asking each member for their individual idea allows the child to **experience responsibility**. The acting out of their suggestion allows them to self-appreciate and enables them to **learn to value the contribution they can bring** to group play.)*

Total time: 45 mins

Parental session

Warm Up: **Name Game**   **5 mins**

Instructions: With the group in a circle facing one another, each member takes a turn to introduce themselves with a movement/action to their name, then the rest of the group copy the action exactly. Example: Alison does a star jump and shouts her name at the same time. The group then copies.

(Purpose of game: This game allows the child to express themselves as an individual. It looks at **multi-task collaboration***; to move; to speak; to think; all at the same time. This game quickly displays those* **with little confidence** *and those who will need extra encouragement.)*

Game 1: **Bake A Cake**   **10 mins**

Instructions: Standing in a circle, ask the children to follow your mime of reaching up, opening a cupboard, getting out the flour and sugar packets and placing them on the imaginary table in front of them. Bend down and open the imaginary fridge; reach for the eggs, milk and butter and place them on the table top. From the imaginary cupboard behind you, get out the mixing bowl and cake tin and place them on top of the table. From the side drawer, get out the spoon and butter knife. Direct the children to mime the following. Placing flour and sugar into a bowl – mix. Breaking the egg, pouring the milk and slicing some butter into the mixing bowl – mix. Ask who can mix the fastest. Ask children to find a special ingredient they would like to add to the mixture. Example: chocolate chips, cherries – mix. Place the mixture into the cake tin then lick the spoon. Say 'yum'. Put on imaginary oven gloves, turn around, set the imaginary timer and oven heat by turning knobs. Place cake tin into the oven. Cross your arms and whistle for time to pass. Sniff the air and ask the children if they can smell their cake cooking. Call out 'ding' to represent the timer; with gloves still on turn off oven, take cake out, blow cake to cool. Place cake on plate and cut a slice to eat. Mime eating cake. Ask children to place the remaining cake by their coats so they remember to take it home at the end of the session. End sitting in circle.

(Purpose of game: The children are asked to follow direction and **improve their attention to detail and focusing skills***. It helps to improve listening skills and* **working as an individual within a group setting***. It also complements fine motor skill development.)*

Exercise 1: **Mirroring Partners**   **10 mins**

Instructions: Ask the group to team up into pairs of similar height. The children then decide who is A and who is B. Facing one another, A copies the moves B makes as if they are looking into a mirror. Small moves are to be encouraged so the copying can be precise. Example: B scratches head and A copies movement exactly. Develop to strong movements such as balancing and synchronised movements. Example: balancing on left leg whilst touching nose with right hand. Swap leaders so B copies A movements. Then try having no leader and use involuntary movements to start the copying process. Example: A looking at B, A fidgets with skirt involuntarily, B copies the fidget movement and, in turn, A copies B, and movement sequence has started.

*(Purpose of exercise: By working in pairs this exercise explores **leadership qualities as well as negotiation skills**. The children will be either encouraged to take the leadership role when usually they prefer not to, or to take a secondary role when they would often volunteer to be the leader. Movement and co-ordination is experimented with through the observation process. This in turn will help to develop the brain's cognitive process through **relaying exact information from sight to movement succinctly** and will further the development of fine motor skills.)*

Exercise 2: **Emotional Statues**   **20 mins**

Instructions: First discuss what an emotion is and the different types we experience. Example: angry, happy, sad etc. Then put the group into smaller groups of either four or five members (see Glossary, Smaller-sized groups). Ask each individual group to create a physical dramatisation of a given emotion with the one rule that everyone must be connected to someone else. The groups are then to prepare a statue of what they believe an emotion could physically look like. Example: angry – each member of the group could place their limbs entwined with each other to represent the feeling of a knotted tangle about to snap under pressure; happy – the idea of floating can be dramatised by holding hands and all leaning slightly backwards and balancing in a state of contentment; sad – create a small ball of everyone hiding behind one another and creating a barrier where no one can see their faces. This can be explored further with more complex emotions such as jealousy, excitement, frustration etc. or by adding slight movement or sounds to the statue. Once the groups have devised their piece, sit the whole group into an audience position and ask them, one by one, to show. After each display discuss why we might feel that way and how we can control that feeling in our everyday lives.

*(Purpose of exercise: This exercise helps to build self-awareness **by translating emotional experiences** into a tangible form. The dramatisation of emotions can help them to **analyse and appreciate feelings** they experience personally. By creating an understanding they can help themselves to break or adapt a pattern of behaviour and build towards **positive social skills**.)*

Total time: 45 mins

Drama Sessions for Primary Schools and Drama Clubs

Parental session: notes

Welcome to our drama session. I thought it would be useful to provide you with a brief outline of the exercises we will be doing today, so you can have a better understanding of our aims and achievements.

Warm Up: **Name Game**

This exercise allows the child to express themselves as an individual. It also looks at multi-task collaboration; to move; to speak; to think; all at the same time.

Game 1: **Bake a Cake**

By following direction the children are improving their attention to detail and focusing skills. It helps to improve listening skills and working as an individual within a group setting. It also develops fine motor skills (small, precise and direct movement).

Exercise 1: **Mirroring Partners**

By working in pairs this exercise explores leadership qualities as well as negotiation skills. The children will be either encouraged to take the leadership role when usually they prefer not to, or to take a secondary role when they would often volunteer to be the leader. You can witness their negotiation skills by watching how they decide who will go first! Movement and co-ordination is developed by the watching and copying process.

Exercise 2: **Emotional Statues**

This exercise helps the children to break down and understand the complex feelings they may experience. It helps them to create an appreciation of how others may feel and develops their personal communication skills. It builds their imagination and story telling skills by translating a feeling into something physical.

Club term 2

Club term 2: 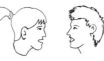 **Session 1 of 11**

Warm Up: **Name Game** 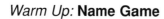 **5 mins**

Instructions: With the group in a circle facing one another, each member takes a turn to introduce themselves with a movement/action to their name, then the rest of the group copy the action exactly. Example: Alison does a star jump and shouts her name at the same time. The group then copies.

*(Purpose of game: This exercise allows the child to express themselves as an individual. It looks at **multi-task collaboration**; to move; to speak; to think; all at the same time. This game quickly displays those with **little confidence** and those who will need extra encouragement.)*

Game 1: **Kabish Kaboo** **10 mins**

Instructions: With the group sitting down, explain that once upon a time there was an island called Kabish Kaboo. On this island lived three creatures: a wizard – *(action)* standing – place arms out in front of you, wiggling fingers; a dwarf – *(action)* crouch to floor with two fingers on head to represent horns; a giant – *(action)* stand on tip toe with upstretched arms. The creatures didn't like each other and when they met one another they would have a battle. There would be a winner and a loser.

- The giant would win over the dwarf: as the giant was so tall all he needed to do was stamp and squash the dwarf flat.
- The wizard would win over the giant, as the wizard could cast a spell to make the giant disappear.
- The dwarf would win over the wizard: as the dwarf was so small the wizard would not notice the dwarf chewing the wizard's ankle and all of his powers draining away.

Now split the group into two separate teams and place them at opposite sides of the space. Elect two team leaders for each team and ask them to decide on a group creature (all team members are to be the same creature). Once decided, the teams line up facing each other and on the direction of the teacher they stride forward calling out 'Kabish Kaboo'. Once at arm's length they stop walking and stand still. Then the teacher shouts 'now' and the two teams display the action of their chosen creature. Depending on whether they are the winners or the losers they either chase after and tag the losers before they reach home or run home as fast as they can to avoid being tagged. Those tagged during the chase then join the opposing team and the game continues. (Note: if the two teams display the same creature, they are to return to their home and decide upon on the next creature.) Repeat approximately ten times. The ultimate winner is the team with the most members.

*(Purpose of game: This game helps to **build team bonding and leadership qualities**. The game can only work properly if every member is fully participating and focused. One member can let the whole side down so **individual responsibility to reach a group goal** is taught.)*

Exercise 1: **Stage Emotions**   **30 mins**

Instructions: Ask the group to sit down in an audience position and select five members to stand before them. Discuss with the group different types of emotions. Example: happy, sad, angry etc. Select one of the emotions and then ask the five members to turn their back to their audience and quietly practise a short display of what that emotion would look like as an action. Example: excitement; to be very smiley, jump up and down on the spot saying 'I can't wait!' On the count of three the members turn around and face their audience and act out the emotion. The audience applaud the performers and then a new selection of members are chosen for the next emotional display. Once everyone has performed an emotion the exercise develops further into the second stage. This time around, the members are to perform the emotion, but also include a story of why they feel this particular way. Example: angry – *(action)* clenched fists, screwed-up face, mumbling words; *(story)* they are feeling angry because their younger brother has just broken their most prized possession and their mother blamed them for leaving it in harm's reach. Continue until everyone has performed an emotion with story to the audience.

*(Purpose of exercise: This exercise uses the tool of acting to **help build confidence and self-analysis**. Thinking through why you feel a certain way creates a **self-awareness**. This in turn helps to build confidence as they learn how to **make a judgement from a set of circumstances** and why they feel a particular way.)*

Total time: 45 mins

Warm Up: **Kabish Kaboo**   **5 mins**

Instructions: With the group sitting down, explain that once upon a time there was an island called Kabish Kaboo. On this island lived three creatures: a wizard – *(action)* standing, place arms out in front of you, wiggling fingers; a dwarf – *(action)* crouch to floor with two fingers on head to represent horns. a giant – *(action)* stand on tip toe with upstretched arms. The creatures didn't like each other and when they met one another they would have a battle. There would be a winner and a loser.

- The giant would win over the dwarf: as the giant was so tall all he needed to do was stamp and squash the dwarf flat.
- The wizard would win over the giant: as the wizard could cast a spell to make the giant disappear.
- The dwarf would win over the wizard: as the dwarf was so small, the wizard would not notice the dwarf chewing the wizard's ankle and all of his powers draining away.

Now split the group into two separate teams and place them at opposite sides of the space. Elect two team leaders for each team and ask them to decide on a group creature (all team members are to be the same creature). Once decided, the teams line up facing towards each other and on the direction of the teacher they stride forward calling out 'Kabish Kaboo'. Once at arm's length, they stop walking and stand still. Then the teacher shouts 'now' and the two teams display the action of their chosen creature. Depending on whether they are the winners or the losers, they either chase after and tag the losers before they reach home or run home as fast as they can to avoid being tagged. Those tagged during the chase then join the opposing team and the game continues. (Note: if the two teams display the same creature, they are to return to their home and decide upon on the next creature.) Repeat approximately ten times. The ultimate winner is the team with the most members.

*(Purpose of game: This game helps to **build team bonding and leadership qualities**. The game can only work properly if every member is fully participating and focused. One member can let the whole side down so **individual responsibility to reach a group goal** is taught.)*

Game 1: **Zip, Zap, Bong!**   **10 mins**

Instructions: With the group in a standing circle explain that the members are all very important transmitters in a power circuit. The electricity can only be transported to one another in the following ways. You can pass the electricity to the people either side of you by placing your hands palm to palm, pointing to them and saying 'zip'. You can only pass the electricity across the circle by

Drama Sessions for Primary Schools and Drama Clubs

placing your hands palm to palm, throwing the ball of power across to an individual and saying 'zap'. You can choose to reject the power being sent to you by doing a star jump and saying 'bong' in the direction it came from. This sends the power back to that person. Members get frazzled by the extreme heat of the electricity if they hold on to it for too long or say the wrong word to the action. Once someone is out, the teacher continues the game by doing the first action. The winner is the last member standing.

*(Purpose of exercise: This game is all about improving **concentration and focus**. The game is fast and unpredictable and this challenges its members into **thinking ahead with quick but calculated reactions**. It teaches responsibility as their attention and focus on the forever-evolving action is the only way they can stay in the game.)*

Exercise 1: **The Photo Game**  **30 mins**

Instructions: With the group in an audience position the teacher explains that they have brought along their imaginary photo album and there are photos of the group inside. Mime getting a particular photo out and show the members, explaining that this photo is of them on the beach. One by one, ask the members to join the acting space in a frozen mime position. Example: sunbathing, building sandcastles, surfing, swimming etc. When half of the group are placed in the photo, the photo is finished. The teacher then calls 'action/freeze' to members, one by one, and they show a mini play (improvisation) to the remaining audience members. Example: the sunbathers apply lotion. The sandcastle is destroyed. The surfer falls off their board. The swimmer starts to drown. Once everyone in the photo has performed individually the whole photo comes to life and a play (improvisation) ensues. The teacher calls a timely 'freeze' and explains the frozen image now in front of them is the photograph previously shown. Repeat.

Photos: **hospital   wedding   theme park   circus   hairdressers**

*(Purpose of exercise: This exercise builds imagination and **storytelling skills**. Showing individual ideas in an improvised context allows a member to **freely express themselves**. It helps build confidence through performing their ideas to others and **being actively praised for their personal efforts**.)*

Total time: 45 mins

Drama Sessions for Primary Schools and Drama Clubs

Warm Up: **Zip, Zap, Bong!**   **5 mins**

Instructions: With the group in a standing circle explain that the members are all very important transmitters in a power circuit. The electricity can only be transported to one another in the following ways. You can pass the electricity to the people either side of you by placing your hands palm to palm, pointing to them and saying 'zip'. You can only pass the electricity across the circle by placing your hands palm to palm, throwing the ball of power across to an individual and saying 'zap'. You can choose to reject the power being sent to you by doing a star jump and saying 'bong' in the direction it came from. This sends the power back to that person. Members get frazzled by the extreme heat of the electricity if they hold on to it for too long or say the wrong word to the action. Once someone is out, the teacher continues the game by doing the first action. The winner is the last member standing.

*(Purpose of exercise: This game is all about improving **concentration and focus**. The game is fast and unpredictable and this challenges its members into **thinking ahead with quick but calculated reactions**. It teaches responsibility as their attention and focus on the forever-evolving action is the only way they can stay in the game.)*

Game 1: **Stuck In the Mud**   **10 mins**

Instructions: Ask the group members to find a space within the room and explain the following rules. One member is chosen to be 'it' and the others are to move around the space trying to avoid being tagged by them. There is no safe home and once tagged they are to freeze on the spot with legs apart. In order to be free to move again, someone has to dive through the legs of the frozen member without being tagged themselves. Gradually, as the game progresses, additional 'it' members join the tagging team and the game concludes once all members have been tagged – hence stuck in the mud.

*(Purpose of game: This game helps to **burn up excess energy** and explores team problem-solving. It shows that working together and **creating a strategy or game plan** will produce faster results.)*

Exercise 1: **Machines**   **30 mins**

Instructions: Place the group into an audience position and explain that the members are all cogs in a working machine. Decide on a machine and then select particular members to join the performance space, one by one, in order to build this chosen machine. Example: bubble-gum-making machine. One member starts the conveyor belt machine by crouching down and placing arms as if a mixing bowl. A second member joins the space with an action of tipping ingredients into the mixing bowl. A third member joins the machine as if a whisk that has different spinning speeds, and so on. Each member must have an action and a sound. When half of the group have joined the performance space the machine should be completed with the last member producing the end-product. If you have a large group, remember the items can be packaged for transportation and deliveries in machine formations can be made. Example: fork-lift truck manoeuvres storing packed boxes. Once the machine is completed and individual actions and sounds have been shown, the teacher mimes flicking the main switch on and the whole machine springs to life, all working together in unison. The teacher then switches the machine off and another machine is then created by new members.

*(Purpose of exercise: This exercise helps to **develop improvisation and communication skills**. The ever-changing formation of the machine encourages the members to **remain flexible** and to develop their ideas from what they see before them. Being able to translate out-of-the-ordinary ideas into a physical form introduces the skill of **effective communication**.)*

Total time: 45 mins

Warm Up: **Stuck in the Mud**   **5 mins**

Instructions: Ask the group members to find a space within the room and explain the following rules. One member is chosen to be 'it' and the others are to move around the space trying to avoid being tagged by them. There is no safe home and once tagged they are to freeze on the spot with legs apart. In order to be free to move again, someone has to dive through the legs of the frozen member without being tagged themselves. Gradually, as the game progresses, additional 'it' members join the tagging team and the game concludes once all members have been tagged – hence stuck in the mud.

*(Purpose of game: This game helps to **burn up excess energy** and explores team problem-solving. It shows that working together and **creating a strategy or game plan** will produce faster results.)*

Game 1: **Hypnosis**   **10 mins**

Instructions: Ask the group to find pairs of similar height. Then the pairs are to decide on a leader and a follower. The leader is to place the palm of their hand approximately 20 cm in front of the follower's face. The leader is to slowly lead the follower around the space, with the aim of the follower keeping the same distance from the palm of the hand at all times. Be sure to encourage the leader to explore height and depth, moving forwards and backwards, as well as along the floor and around in circles. Change roles and repeat.

*(Purpose of game: This game explores **physical posture and experimental movement of the body**. It also introduces **submissive and controlling emotions**, and how it can feel to be manipulated and helpless as well as over-bearing and demanding. Experimenting with extreme emotions helps to create a further understanding of **self-awareness**.)*

Exercise 1: **Story Line-by-Line**   **30 mins**

Instructions: With the group sitting in a circle explain that you are about to create a story sentence by sentence. Each member is to add a sentence that builds a whole story going around the circle. Example: Member 1 – Once upon a time there was a cat stuck up a tree; Member 2 – The cat miaowed for help to a passer-by; Member 3 – The passer-by was an old lady on her way to the shops; Member 4 – The old lady noticed the stuck cat and attempted to call the fire brigade on her mobile phone; Member 5 – When suddenly she noticed she had no battery charge . . . etc. When you approach the last few members of the circle, be sure the story concludes and ends with 'The end'. Now the group is to act out the devised story, so be sure to either take notes or remember the order of action. Cast the roles, place the scenes about the space and the

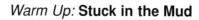

teacher narrates the story to give it order and organisation. Repeat with a new circle story.

*(Purpose of exercise: This exercise firstly **challenges concentration and patience**. Waiting turn to tell an idea that may have evolved several times as the story unfolds stretches the patience level to its maximum. Having to fully concentrate on the story and remember the sequences of action so you can play the cast role effectively develops listening and information retention skills. Secondly, it encourages further **development of literacy skills** by under-standing ideas, building stories and developing descriptive language. Thirdly, it allows members to act out **a performance devised and created as a team but contains their personal input**.)*

Total time: 45 mins

Session materials: newspaper photographs

Warm Up: **Hypnosis**   **5 mins**

Instructions: Ask the group to find pairs of similar height. Then the pairs are to decide on a leader and a follower. The leader is to place the palm of their hand approximately 20 cm in front of the follower's face. The leader is to slowly lead the follower around the space, with the aim of the follower keeping the same distance from the palm of the hand at all times. Be sure to encourage the leader to explore height and depth, moving forwards and backwards, as well as along the floor and around in circles. Change roles and repeat.

*(Purpose of game: This game explores **physical posture and experimental movement of the body**. It also introduces **submissive and controlling emotions**, and how it can feel to be manipulated and helpless as well as over-bearing and demanding. Experimenting with extreme emotions helps to create a further understanding of **self-awareness**.)*

Game 1: **Lead the Blind**   **10 mins**

Instructions: Ask the group to get in similar-height pairs but with someone they haven't worked with before. Ask the pair to decide on an A and a B. A is to lead B around the space by controlling them through touch alone. A is to hold their palm out flat and B is to place their palm on top. Standing close to one another, B is then asked to close their eyes and, through sensory touch alone, they are guided around the space slowly and carefully. When A stops, B is to stop immediately. When A turns left or right the palm should indicate this by an adjustment of the wrist accordingly. Swap roles and repeat.

*(Purpose of game: This game introduces the **social skill of trust**. Learning to build trust in others takes great courage and only through example and play can this be achieved. This game allows the trust skill to be developed by showing that leaning on others during a time of need and feeling strong enough to ask for help is socially acceptable.)*

Exercise 1: **Newspaper Clippings**   **30 mins**

Instructions: Place the members into smaller groups (see Glossary, Smaller-sized groups) and hand each group a selected photo from a newspaper. The newspaper photo should have no caption or news details, and ideally should include a group of people. Explain the groups are to reproduce the photo by placing themselves in the space as a frozen image. They are then to create and devise a story that follows on from the photo to perform to the rest of the group. Example: photo is of an award ceremony. Frozen Image: people place

Drama Sessions for Primary Schools and Drama Clubs

themselves in the space as if on a podium about to receive awards like the photo suggests. Story and action: suddenly the judge realises the golden cup is a fake and has been swapped for the real one. An investigation and accusations ensue. Once the mini plays have been devised, ask each group to perform to the remaining members in audience position.

*(Purpose of exercise: This exercise continues to develop the **storytelling skill** and development of the imagination. Using the photo source as a building platform **allows constructive, experimental, free-flowing individual thoughts** that can be juxtaposed to make a group story. It also explores team role play as being able to effectively work in a group under time constraints and with pressure to achieve an end-product successfully shows **that each individual member has a duty to their group and to make a valuable contribution.**)*

Total time: 45 mins

Drama Sessions for Primary Schools and Drama Clubs

Session materials: Blindfold

Warm Up: **Lead the Blind**   **5 mins**

Instructions: Ask the group to get in similar-height pairs but with someone they haven't worked with before. Ask the pair to decide on an A and a B. A is to lead B around the space by controlling them through touch alone. A is to hold their palm out flat and B is to place their palm on top. Standing close to one another, B is then asked to close their eyes and, through sensory touch alone, they are guided around the space slowly and carefully. When A stops, B is to stop immediately. When A turns left or right the palm should indicate this by an adjustment of the wrist accordingly. Swap roles and repeat.

*(Purpose of game: This game introduces the **social skill of trust**. Learning to build trust in others takes great courage and only through example and play can this be achieved. This game allows the trust skill to be developed by showing that leaning on others during a time of need and feeling strong enough to ask for help is socially acceptable.)*

Game 1: **Feeling Game**   **10 mins**

Instructions: The group forms a circle and one member is chosen to be blind-folded. This person is then gently spun around and let loose to walk into a standing member. The blindfolded person then feels the face of that member to guess who they are. If they guess correctly it is that member's turn to be blind-folded. If they guess incorrectly they are to move on to another person to guess again.

*(Purpose of game: This game attempts to **break inhibitions** by allowing the embarrassment of touch to be explored through a fun game. It also **enhances sensory recognition** and the development of **recall memory** through game play.)*

Exercise 1: **Confused Nursery Rhymes**   **30 mins**

Instructions: Put the members into smaller groups with a team leader (see Glossary, Smaller-sized groups) and explain that they are to create and practise a short play to show the rest of the group based upon a well-known nursery rhyme of their choice. However, each group must decide on a different ending to that which is traditionally known. Example: Humpty Dumpty had the great fall but a very clever surgeon who was a personal friend of the King could put Humpty together again by enhanced plastic surgery and limb implants. The more imaginative the better. The devising (making-up) process should take no longer than 15 mins as time will be needed to perform to each other. Once the devising time has passed, ask the members to sit in an audience position but still in their smaller groups to retain concentration. Show each performance and praise all efforts.

*(Purpose of exercise: This exercise introduces **team role play and negotiation skills**. Working with a team leader puts responsibility on one member to manage and succeed in completing the task. Negotiation skills are explored by all members in order to get their ideas and suggestions put forward for group discussion. Handling personal rejection (through ideas not being deemed successful) **allows the members to develop emotionally**. Organisational skills are explored through time constraints and working together as a whole unit to get a rehearsed performance completed. Besides all of these factors the idea of not performing the traditional ending **allows free expression and exploration of creative thought**.)*

Total time: 45 mins

Session materials: Blindfold

Warm Up: **Feeling Game**   **5 mins**

Instructions: The group forms a circle and one member is chosen to be blind-folded. This person is then gently spun around and let loose to walk into a standing member. The blindfolded person then feels the face of that member to guess who they are. If they guess correctly it is then that member's turn to be blindfolded. If they guess incorrectly they are to move on to another person to guess again.

*(Purpose of game: This game attempts to **break inhibitions** by allowing the embarrassment of touch to be explored through a fun game. It also **enhances sensory recognition** and the development of **recall memory** through game play.)*

Game 1: **Traffic Lights**   **10 mins**

Instructions: The group are to move around the space in three different ways. When the teacher calls out RED the members are to stand still (frozen). When AMBER is called the children are to walk as fast as possible. When GREEN is called the children are to run as fast as they can around the space without bumping into anyone or anything. The teacher can then choose to allocate the calling of colours to different members of the group.

*(Purpose of game: This game helps to focus the group for further activity and **strengthen concentration levels**. It also helps to burn up any excess energy and develops a **team ethos**.)*

Exercise 1: **Key Words**   **30 mins**

Instructions: Place the group into smaller groups (see Glossary, Smaller-sized groups) each with a new team leader. Then hand each group a key word from which they are to create and rehearse a short play to show the rest of the group. The key word should be the platform on which they base their play. Example: keyword = 'shipwrecked': The story starts with two members making a camp-fire on a presumed desert island. During the late evening they hear strange noises and go to investigate. They discover a group of tribal dancers perform-ing a ritual rain dance when suddenly they are discovered and captured . . . etc. Allow 15 minutes devising time and then ask the groups to come together in audience position to show their plays to the rest of the group. Ask for the groups to sit together in order to retain concentration and focus.

Key words: **shipwrecked   robbery   airport   interview   lottery ticket**

*(Purpose of exercise: Again this exercise introduces **team role play and further negotiation skills**. Working with a new team leader allows a different member to experience the responsibility to manage and succeed in completing the task. Further negotiation skills are explored by all members through voicing of their ideas, as is personal rejection if their idea is deemed unsuitable. Organisational skills are explored again through time constraints and working together to get a rehearsed performance completed. Using the key word as a platform **allows the group to remain focused and forward-thinking**, rather than an ideas pot that leaves random ideas pasted together in a blur.)*

Total time: 45 mins

Session materials: 6 different objects

Warm Up: **Traffic Lights** **5 mins**

Instructions: The group are to move around the space in three different ways. When the teacher calls out RED the members are to stand still (frozen). When AMBER is called the children are to walk as fast as possible. When GREEN is called the children are to run as fast as they can around the space without bumping into anyone or anything. The teacher can then choose to allocate the calling of colours to different members of the group.

(Purpose of game: This game helps to focus the group for further activity and **strengthen concentration levels**. *It also helps to burn up any excess energy and develops a* **team ethos**.*)*

Game 1: **Man the Ship** **10 mins**

Instructions: Explain to the group that they are all sailors working together on a ship. There are several commands to which they are to perform an action. These commands are:

'Captain's coming' *(action: to stand up straight with hand salute).*

'Climb the rigging' *(action: to imitate climbing up a rope ladder).*

'Ship is sinking' *(action: to get into pairs sitting back-to-back and imitate rowing a boat).*

'Scrub the decks' *(action: to get on hands and knees and mime washing the floor with a scrubbing brush).*

'Port' *(action: to run to an allocated side of the space).*

'Starboard' *(action: to run to the opposite side of the space).*

Select different members to call out a command and the group performs the action together.

(Purpose of game: This game introduces **working with a set of rules and procedures** *in a fun context. Experiencing rules and guidelines in a gaming format shows that there is always room for* **self-expression**, *but within its boundaries and context. Working as an individual but linked with a team goal helps to* **appreciate self-worth and importance**.*)*

Drama Sessions for Primary Schools and Drama Clubs

Exercise 1: **Short Stories with Props (Part 1)** **30 mins**

Instructions: Ask the group to sit in audience position and place a chair in front of the group. Explain that the chair is the 'storytelling chair' and pick one member to sit on it to become the 'storyteller'. Then select five other members to be 'actors' and to stand facing the audience. The storyteller then chooses one item from the 'bag of props' and quickly thinks of a story based upon that chosen prop. The storyteller then casts each standing member into a role that will help tell the story to the audience. Example: Storyteller picks out a candle from the props bag. They cast Member 1 as a witch, Member 2 as the witch's cat, Member 3 as a wizard, Member 4 as a boy and Member 5 as a shopkeeper. The storyteller then either hands the prop to an actor or places it within the performance space in relation to their story. Then the storyteller starts to tell their story and as the action is read the actors perform it to the audience. Be sure that all actors repeat the words the storyteller says that relate to them. Repeat by selecting new storytellers and performers. Try to have all members experience the acting role before the end of the session otherwise disappoint-ment may be felt by those who feel they have missed out. So timekeeping is essential with shorter stories told if necessary.

*(Purpose of exercise: This exercise is designed to **build confidence** through performing to others. The fact that the performers aren't relying on themselves to produce the ideas means they have an invisible crutch to lean on or a mask to hide behind. This in turn breeds confidence and encourages them to stand in front of others and perform, as they are not fully disclosing themselves and lose the fear of rejection. The skill of **listening and relaying information** is also explored by the performers and further development of **literacy skills** is experienced by the storyteller through learning to build a cohesive story line within minutes.)*

Total time: 45 mins

Session materials: 6 different masks

Warm up: **Man the Ship**   **5 mins**

Instructions: Explain to the group that they are all sailors working together on a ship. There are several commands to which they are to perform an action. These commands are:

'Captain's coming' *(action: to stand up straight with hand salute).*

'Climb the rigging' *(action: to imitate climbing up a rope ladder).*

'Ship is sinking' *(action: to get into pairs sitting back-to-back and imitate rowing a boat).*

'Scrub the decks' *(action: to get on hands and knees and mime washing the floor with a scrubbing brush).*

'Port' *(action: to run to an allocated side of the space).*

'Starboard' *(action: to run to the opposite side of the space).*

Select different members to call out a command and the group performs the action together.

*(Purpose of game: This game introduces **working with a set of rules and procedures** in a fun context. Experiencing rules and guidelines in a gaming format shows that there is always room for **self-expression**, but within its boundaries and context. Working as an individual but linked with a team goal helps to **appreciate self-worth and importance**.)*

Game 1: **Cat and Mouse**   **10 mins**

Instructions: Ask the group to get together into teams of three and to then find a space within the room. Explain that they are to stand with linked arms to represent a wall. Then choose one member to be the cat and another to be the mouse. The cat chases after the mouse and the mouse gets safe by joining to an end of a wall. This in turn makes the opposite member of the wall the new mouse, which the cat then chases. If the cat is fast enough to catch the mouse the roles reverse and the cat becomes the mouse and attempts to get safe by joining a wall. The mouse then is the new cat. To add further game play you can choose to include more sets of cats and mice, but be sure that the cats only chase their elected mouse and do not cross over as this will cause confusion and the game will cease.

*(Purpose of game: This game introduces **strategic planning within game play**. The action is fast and ever-changing and this demands focus and full*

Drama Sessions for Primary Schools and Drama Clubs

*attention at all times for all members. The game requires **problem-solving and quick reactions**, but no one is ever caught out so the **feeling of inclusion and succeeding** is experienced by everyone.)*

Exercise 1: **Short Stories with Masks (Part 2)**   **30 mins**

Instructions: Ask the group to sit in audience position and place a chair in front of the group. Explain that you are to repeat a similar exercise that was done last week but with a slight difference. Again the chair is the 'storytelling chair' and select a new member to sit on it to become the 'storyteller'. Then select five other members to be 'actors' and to stand facing the audience. The storyteller then chooses one mask from the 'bag of props' and quickly thinks of a story based upon that chosen mask. The storyteller then casts each standing member into a role that will help tell the story to the audience. Example: Storyteller picks out a chicken mask from the props bag. They cast Member 1 as a chicken, Member 2 as a farmer, Member 3 as a farmer's wife, Member 4 as a fox, Member 5 as a vet. The storyteller then hands the mask to the actor in relation to their story. Then the storyteller starts to tell their story and as the action is read the actors perform it to the audience. Be sure that all actors repeat the words the storyteller says that relates to them. Repeat by selecting new storytellers and performers. Again, try to have all members experience the acting role before the end of the session otherwise disappointment may be felt by those who feel they have missed out. So timekeeping is essential with shorter stories told if necessary.

*(Purpose of exercise: Repeating this exercise allows members who did not get the chance to sit on the storytelling chair the previous week **a chance to experience the task**. This further develops confidence as maybe those who did not feel confident enough to attempt it last week may do this week. Hopefully, you will also **experience a progression in the quality of stories produced**, as witnessing the better examples will further the weaker ones.)*

Total time: 45 mins

Session materials: 6 different hats

Warm up: **Cat and Mouse**   **5 mins**

Instructions: Ask the group to get together into teams of three and to then find a space within the room. Explain that they are to stand with linked arms to represent a wall. Then choose one member to be the cat and another to be the mouse. The cat chases after the mouse and the mouse gets safe by joining to an end of a wall. This in turn makes the opposite member of the wall the new mouse, which the cat then chases. If the cat is fast enough to catch the mouse the roles reverse and the cat becomes the mouse and attempts to get safe by joining a wall. The mouse is then the new cat. To add further game play you can choose to include more sets of cats and mice, but be sure that the cats only chase their elected mouse and do not cross over as this will cause confusion and the game will cease.

*(Purpose of game: This game introduces **strategic planning within game play**. The action is fast and ever-changing and this demands focus and full attention at all times for all members. The game requires **problem-solving and quick reactions**, but no one is ever caught out so the **feeling of inclusion and succeeding** is experienced by everyone.)*

Game 1: **Teacher Says**    **10 mins**

Instructions: With the group standing in a circle explain that a series of instructions will be given to the members. They must follow the instructions if the nominated member says the Teacher tells them to. Example: Member 1 says: 'Teacher says put your hands on your head'. The group then completes the action. Member 1 then says: 'Teacher says put your hands on your knees'. The group then completes the action. However, if the action is called without 'Teacher says' and members complete the action, those members sit out within the circle. Example: Member 1 says: 'Balance on one leg' and some members do so, they are out of the game. Select different members to be the teacher.

*(Purpose of game: This game **stimulates listening skills** and demonstrates to members the importance of listening carefully. The game keeps the group focused but in an active concentrated way.)*

Exercise 1: **Short Stories with Hats (Part 3)**   **30 mins**

Instructions: Ask the group to sit in an audience position and place a chair in front of the group. Explain that you are to repeat the exercise that was done last week but again with a slight difference. Place a chair in front of the group and explain that it is the 'storytelling chair' and select a new member to sit on it to

Drama Sessions for Primary Schools and Drama Clubs

become the 'storyteller'. Then select five other members to be 'actors' and to stand facing the audience. The storyteller then chooses one hat from the bag of props and quickly thinks of a story based upon that chosen hat. The storyteller then casts each standing member into a role that will help tell the story to the audience. Example: Storyteller picks out a crown from the props bag. They cast Member 1 as a king, Member 2 as a queen, Member 3 as a knight, Member 4 as a dragon, Member 5 as a horse. The storyteller then hands the crown to the actor in relation to their story. Then the storyteller starts to tell their story and as the action is read the actors perform it to the audience. Be sure that all actors repeat the words the storyteller says that relates to them. Repeat by selecting new storytellers and performers. Again, try to have all members experience the acting role before the end of the session otherwise disappointment may be felt by those who feel they have missed out. So time keeping is essential with shorter stories told if necessary.

*(Purpose of exercise: Repeating this exercise is purely about creating equality and allowing all members to experience the task of telling a story. Further development in literacy skills should prevail where **the stories should now be of calibre** and the actual performing should be to a reasonable standard.)*

Total time: 45 mins

Drama Sessions for Primary Schools and Drama Clubs

Parental session

Session materials: 2 objects, 2 masks, 2 hats

Warm Up: **Name Game**   **5 mins**

Instructions: With the group in a circle facing one another, each member takes a turn to introduce themselves with a movement/action to their name, then the rest of the group copy the action exactly. Example: Alison does a star jump and shouts her name at the same time. The group then copies.

*(Purpose of game: This game allows the child to express themselves as an individual. It looks at **multi-task collaboration**; to move; to speak; to think; all at the same time. This game quickly displays those **with little confidence** and those who will need extra encouragement.)*

Game 1: **Zip, Zap, Bong!**   **10 mins**

Instructions: With the group in a standing circle explain that the members are all very important transmitters in a power circuit. The electricity can only be transported to one another in the following ways. You can pass the electricity to the people either side of you by placing your hands palm to palm, pointing to them and saying 'zip'. You can only pass the electricity across the circle by placing your hands palm to palm, throwing the ball of power across to an individual and saying 'zap'. You can choose to reject the power being sent to you by doing a star jump and saying 'bong' in the direction it came from. This sends the power back to that person. Members get frazzled by the extreme heat of the electricity if they hold on to it for too long or say the wrong word to the action. Once someone is out, the teacher continues the game by doing the first action. The winner is the last member standing.

*(Purpose of exercise: This game is all about improving **concentration and focus**. The game is fast and unpredictable and this challenges its members into **thinking ahead with quick but calculated reactions**. It teaches responsibility as their attention and focus on the forever-evolving action is the only way they can stay in the game.)*

Exercise 1: **Short Stories with**
                     Props/Masks/Hats   **30 mins**

Instructions: Ask the group to sit in audience position and place a chair in front of the group and watching parents. Explain that the chair is the 'storytelling chair' and pick one member to sit on it and become the 'storyteller'. Then select five other members to be 'actors' and to stand facing the audience. The storyteller then chooses one item from the bag of props and quickly thinks of a story based upon that chosen prop. The storyteller then casts each standing member into a role that will help tell the story to the audience. Example: Storyteller picks out a candle from the props bag. They cast Member 1 as a witch, Member 2 as a witch's cat, Member 3 as a wizard, Member 4 as a boy, Member 5 as a shopkeeper. The storyteller then either hands the prop to an actor or places it within the performance space in relation to their story. Then the storyteller starts to tell their story and as the action is read the actors perform it to the audience. Be sure that all actors repeat the words the story-teller says that relate to them. Repeat by selecting new storytellers and performers. It is essential to have all members experience the acting role before the end of the session to avoid disappointment being felt by those who feel they have missed out. So timekeeping is essential with shorter stories told if necessary.

(Purpose of exercise: By choosing to show this exercise you continue to build the children's **confidence** *as they are now performing to adults, but still within a safe, known environment and format. It also helps the adults to see their child's personal development and* **how drama has helped build creative imagination, structured gaming and excitable but self-controlled children***.)*

Total time: 45 mins

Drama Sessions for Primary Schools and Drama Clubs

Parental session: notes

Welcome to our drama session. I thought it would be useful to provide you with a brief outline of the exercises we will be doing today, so you can have a better understanding of our aims and achievements.

Warm Up: **Name Game**

This exercise allows the child to express themselves as an individual. It also looks at multi-task collaboration; to move; to speak; to think; all at the same time.

Game 1: **Zip, Zap, Bong!**

This game helps to build concentration levels and focus. The fun interactive rules help keep the child focused on the action. If they switch off, even for a second, they are caught out.

Exercise 1: **Stories and Props**

This exercise is designed to build confidence through performing to others. The storyteller has the most responsibility in having to produce a cohesive story line within minutes and this in turn also helps with the development of their literacy skills. Acting on the spot with no rehearsal or planning takes great confidence and the performers get the chance to experience the skill of listening and relaying information through storytelling.

Club term 3

Session materials: blindfold, keys

Warm Up: **Name Game – Version 2**   **5 mins**

Instructions: With the group in a circle facing one another, each member takes a turn to introduce themselves with a movement/action to their name, then the rest of the group copy the action exactly. The next person chosen is selected by the previous member. Example: Alison does a star jump and shouts her name at the same time. The group then copies. Alison then selects Timothy to go next to which the group then copies.

*(Purpose of game: This game allows the child to express themselves as an individual. It looks at **multi-task collaboration**; to move; to speak; to think; all at the same time. This game quickly displays those **with little confidence** and those who will need extra encouragement.)*

Game 1: **Gibberish with Translator**   **10 mins**

Instructions: Sitting in a circle, ask three members to stand up to play. Explain that two members are to talk gibberish (a language of noises and sounds) to each other with animated actions whilst the third member translates the conversation into English for the rest of the group. Of course, there is no planning and the translator just explains what they believe the conversation is about. The group take turns to play until all have contributed.

*(Purpose of game: This game is just a further introduction to **breaking inhibitions and building confidence**. Having the added element of translator allows the body language displayed by the talking members analysed and interpreted. By doing this we show the watching members that we often **provide non-verbal communication through involuntary and voluntary body movement/language**.)*

Exercise 1: **Head Space**      **10 mins**

Instructions: Ask the group to find a space within the room and start to walk slowly around. Then the teacher calls out instructions, which the group are to follow. The instructions are based on a number and an ensemble, and whilst they are grouping themselves together they are not allowed to stop walking. Examples are:

    three members; to hold hands.
    two members; one blonde and one brown hair.
    four members; holding waists.
    two members; one brown, one blue eyes.

three members; two girls, one boy.

four members; two skirts, two trousers.

*(Purpose of this exercise: This game helps to show members how to keep thinking and focused under stressful circumstances. With people moving and instructions constantly changing, this fun game helps to develop the **skill of problem-solving under pressure**. It teaches how not to give up and how concentration and **thinking things through can help to achieve** things.)*

Exercise 2: **Keeper and the Keys**      **20 mins**

Instructions: Place one chair in the middle of the space and ask the group to sit opposite it at one end of the room. Place the keys under the chair. Explain that once upon a time a king needed to keep the keys to his treasure safe and appointed a guard to protect them. However, this was no ordinary guard, this guard was blind. The king believed that the blind guard's hearing would be much better than anyone else's and he would catch any intruder. Pick one member to sit on the chair and blindfold them. Explain that a member will be selected to move across the space and attempt to steal the keys from underneath the chair. The guard can catch the thief by pointing in the direction they believe them to be. The guard cannot make sweeping movements but can finger-point to a given location. If the thief is caught, they sit back down and another person attempts it. If the thief is successful by grabbing the keys undetected they get to sit on the chair and be blindfolded. Be sure to encourage the members to be inventive as to how best to cross the space without being caught.

*(Purpose of exercise: This game continues to explore listening skills. It is believed that by taking away a sense (sight) the remaining senses can over-compensate, and this **exercise allows the members to directly feel that change**. It also looks at how **we perceive personal differences and how we should embrace and not discriminate against individual qualities**. It challenges **group listening skills** as this game can only work if the whole group remains committed to each other and does not hinder the process by making noises distracting. It encourages the members **to think outside the box and be inventive** as to how best to cross the space without being caught.)*

Total time: 45 mins

Session materials: blindfold

Warm Up: **Name Game – Version 2** 5 mins

Instructions: With the group in a circle facing one another, each member takes a turn to introduce themselves with a movement/action to their name, then the rest of the group copy the action exactly. The next person chosen is selected by the previous member. Example: Alison does a star jump and shouts her name at the same time. The group then copies. Alison then selects Timothy to go next to which the group then copies.

*(Purpose of game: This game allows the child to express themselves as an individual. It looks at **multi-task collaboration**; to move; to speak; to think; all at the same time. This game quickly displays those **with little confidence** and those who will need extra encouragement.)*

Game 1: **Feared but Protected** 10 mins

Instructions: Ask the group to space out within the room. Then ask each member to secretly select a member from the group to be someone they fear. Then ask each member to secretly select another member who will protect them. Now ask everyone to move about the space keeping the protector between themselves and those feared. Example: Lynn chooses Stuart to be the one she fears. She moves about the space to keep Sandra, her chosen protector, between Stuart and herself. It is important that the members do not express their chosen markers as unnecessary alienation can be created.

*(Purpose of game: This game helps to experiment with **spacial awareness** and helps to focus the mind. It creates **controlled tension** and explores an **avenue for safe release**.)*

Game 2: **Random Counting** 5 mins

Instructions: Ask the group to sit in a circle and then to face out into the space (not face into the circle as usual). With their backs to each other, the teacher explains that the group will attempt to count to 20 spontaneously and at random. Example: One member starts by calling out number 1. Then a different member calls out number 2. A third member then calls out number 3 . . . etc. It is never discussed or pre-planned as to who will call out the next number. Once a member has called out a number they are not to call out again. If two people shout out at the same time the group has to start the counting all over again. Note the highest number achieved for future reference.

Drama Sessions for Primary Schools and Drama Clubs

*(Purpose of exercise: This game creates **team cohesion** and working together to achieve an end goal. It helps show the group how much of a united front they can be and how listening and perceiving others' actions can help them to make useful judgements. It will also show some members how easily they can become frustrated as unsuccessful attempts will trigger certain members' disappointment.)*

Exercise 1: **Adam and Eve**  **25 mins**

Instructions: Ask the group to create a rectangle (rather than a circle) and ask them to sit with their legs crossed and arms out with palms facing forward to create a barrier of protection. Then select two members to be blindfolded and place them in the middle of the rectangle. The two members are only allowed to move around the rectangle on their hands and knees. One member is called Adam and they are to try to catch the other member called Eve. Eve is to try to escape the touch of Adam. The game begins with Adam and Eve at opposite ends of the rectangle with the remaining group members being silent and protecting Adam and Eve from heading out of the rectangle by gently guiding them back inwards with their hands.

*(Purpose of exercise: This exercise again looks at **sensory skills and the use of heightening senses** by taking one away. It also looks at listening skills and the recognition of perceiving someone is close by. **Team spirit** is built by looking after and supporting the members conducting the exercise. It provides great **enjoyment through observing others** and making judgements from what they see before them.)*

Total time: 45 mins

Drama Sessions for Primary Schools and Drama Clubs

Warm Up: **Name Game – Version 2** **5 mins**

Instructions: With the group in a circle facing one another, each member takes a turn to introduce themselves with a movement/action to their name, then the rest of the group copy the action exactly. The next person chosen is selected by the previous member. Example: Alison does a star jump and shouts her name at the same time. The group then copies. Alison then selects Timothy to go next to which the group then copies.

*(Purpose of game: This game allows the child to express themselves as an individual. It looks at **multi-task collaboration**; to move; to speak; to think; all at the same time. This game quickly displays those **with little confidence** and those who will need extra encouragement.)*

Game 1: **Blind Car** **10 mins**

Instructions: Ask the group to get into pairs of similar height. Ask the pairs to decide who will be the driver and who will be the car. The driver will control the car by touching the member's back with their fingers. Explain that the driver should press the left shoulder blade to make the car turn left and the right shoulder blade to make the car turn right. To go straight forward the driver presses the centre of the back, and to reverse, the driver presses the lower back. Depending on how hard the driver presses the back depends on the speed of the car. Encourage the group not to race their cars around the space and to think more about the detail of the game. Swap roles and repeat.

*(Purpose of game: This game allows the group to focus and further **their appreciation of non-verbal communication skills**. Creating **working partnerships** helps to encourage and build group bonding and the importance of **a positive group ethos**.)*

Game 2: **Random Counting** **5 mins**

Instructions: Ask the group to sit in a circle and then to face out into the space (not face into the circle as usual). With their backs to each other, the teacher explains that the group will attempt to count to 20 spontaneously and at random. Example: One member starts by calling out number 1. Then a different member calls out number 2. A third member then calls out number 3 . . . etc. It is never discussed or pre-planned as to who will call out the next number. Once a member has called out a number they are not to call out again. If two people shout out at the same time the group has to start the counting all over again. Note the highest number achieved for future reference.

*(Purpose of game: Repeating this game hopes to improve on the previous score and further **builds team cohesion**. It will also allow those who previously experienced outbursts of frustration the chance to focus that energy into concentrating and **trying to achieve the group goal**.)*

Exercise 1: **Party People**   **25 mins**

Instructions: Ask the group to sit in an audience position and select six members to stand up in the performing area. Ask one member to select a piece of paper from an envelope in order to obtain a selection of the community at random (see below). Then ask the performers to begin a spontaneous play (improvisation) based on this group at a party. Example: Elderly people enjoying a sing-song at a party in a nursing home. Toddlers having a tea party at nursery. It is important to encourage the members to act out typical mannerisms and how they believe they would act. Examples: elderly people trying to sing and teeth falling out; toddlers having a food fight. Be sure to explain at the end of the session that everyone is an individual and not a cloned copy of what we may perceive them to be.

**elderly people   toddlers   poor students
posh people   nosey neighbours**

*(Purpose of exercise: This exercise looks at **stereotypes and perceptions**. The game uses the tool of sectioning the community to show how we think about others and how we may observe them. It helps to bring about awareness of others and how we should evaluate our judgements. This in turn helps **build social skills** and how to make independent decisions by **questioning preconceptions** and not necessarily being led by others' judgements.)*

Total time: 45 mins

Warm Up: **Name Game – Version 2** 5 mins

Instructions: With the group in a circle facing one another, each member takes a turn to introduce themselves with a movement/action to their name, then the rest of the group copy the action exactly. The next person chosen is selected by the previous member. Example: Alison does a star jump and shouts her name at the same time. The group then copies. Alison then selects Timothy to go next to which the group then copies.

*(Purpose of game: This game allows the child to express themselves as an individual. It looks at **multi-task collaboration**; to move; to speak; to think; all at the same time. This game quickly displays those **with little confidence** and those who will need extra encouragement.)*

Game 1: **Random Counting – Repeat** 5 mins

Instructions: Ask the group to sit in a circle and then to face out into the space (not face into the circle as usual). With their backs to each other, the teacher explains that the group will attempt to count to 20 spontaneously and at random. Example: One member starts by calling out number 1. Then a different member calls out number 2. A third member then calls out number 3 . . . etc. It is never discussed or pre-planned as to who will call out the next number. Once a member has called out a number they are not to call out again. If two people shout out at the same time the group has to start the counting all over again. Note the highest number achieved for future reference.

*(Purpose of game: Repeating this game is about showing a **commitment** to achieving better results through experiencing **determination and dedication** with the aim to achieve the best group score.)*

Game 2: **Word Tennis** 5 mins

Instructions: Ask the members to find a group of three and sit down facing each other. Explain they are to build a conversation word by word, taking it in turns to say a word each. The sentences and conversation grow depending on the last word spoken. Example: Member 1 says *Hello*, Member 2 says *my*, Member 3 says *friend*, Member 1 says *how*, Member 2 says *are*, Member 3 says *you* . . . etc.

*(Purpose of game: This game helps to **build story lines** and develops the thought processes of **pre-empting what might come next**. This in turn helps improve **improvisation** skills and create a more knowledgeable stage performer.)*

Drama Sessions for Primary Schools and Drama Clubs

Exercise 1: **True Stories** **30 mins**

Instructions: Ask the group to get into pairs and find a space to sit down. Then ask each member to tell their partner a short but detailed true story about themselves. You can guide/influence these true stories to adopt any theme such as vulnerability or loss (if incorporating SEAL topics) or leave to the author's choice for freedom of expression. The partner who is listening has to remember the details of the story and study the mannerisms accompany it. Then ask the whole group to find a space sitting alone. One by one, choose members to stand up and retell their partner's story as if it was from their own personal experience. Encourage the acting to be naturalistic and acute in detail. If the member forgets details ask them to not show this and to continue with what they can remember.

*(Purpose of exercise: This exercise looks at **retaining and relaying information precisely**. Studying the mannerisms and body language relating to someone's personal experience helps the performer to **appreciate and value someone else's perspective**. Retelling that experience in someone else's words and acting as if it was your own produces an in-depth appreciation of what it is like to be someone else.)*

Total time: 45 mins

Drama Sessions for Primary Schools and Drama Clubs

Club term 3:   **Session 5 of 11**

Session materials: large ball

Warm Up: **Name Game – Version 2**   **5 mins**

Instructions: With the group in a circle facing one another, each member takes a turn to introduce themselves with a movement/action to their name, then the rest of the group copy the action exactly. The next person chosen is selected by the previous member. Example: Alison does a star jump and shouts her name at the same time. The group then copies. Alison then selects Timothy to go next to which the group then copies.

*(Purpose of game: This game allows the child to express themselves as an individual. It looks at **multi-task collaboration**; to move; to speak; to think; all at the same time. This game quickly displays those **with little confidence** and those who will need extra encouragement.)*

Game 1: **Name Volley**   **5 mins**

Instructions: Explain that the group are to keep the ball up in the air with volley-style hits. As each member hits the ball, they are to shout out their name. Once the group is managing the task well, swap the names for numbers and ask the group to count in unison. Once the ball touches the ground, the counting has to start from the beginning again.

*(Purpose of game: This game helps to create a team spirit and a positive atmosphere. Helping and **supporting fellow members to achieve success** boosts morale and makes everyone's contribution a valued asset.)*

Exercise 1: **Visit the Zoo**   **35 mins**

Instructions: Explain that the group will take part in a group improvisation. The teacher becomes the narrator and guides the action along to make a group performance. Cast a member to be a bus driver and place a chair in the space. Guide the members into boarding the bus and purchasing a ticket from the driver to the zoo. Ask the members to sit as if they were on a bus, in pairs on the floor, and mime the bus movement. Nominate a member to press the bell to get off at the bus stop for the zoo and all depart. Then split the group into two smaller groups. Ask one to arrange itself at one end of the working space in a frozen-style image of a caged animal. Example: monkeys. Cast the other group as tourists and ask it to place itself around the animals. Call 'Action', and the caged animals come to life. The tourists react accordingly. Example: taking photos of the animals, trying to feed the animals through the bars of the cage … etc. Then shout 'Freeze'. Swap the roles around by now giving the tourists the role of different caged animals and the animals the role of tourists.

76

Repeat. End the improvisation with everyone returning home on the bus and waving goodbye to each other.

Caged animals:

monkeys   penguins   flamingos   elephants   lions   crocodiles

*(Purpose of exercise: This exercise allows the group to experience the feeling of **performing as a company**. Having everyone immersed in the action at the same time allows mini improvisations to naturally evolve. Expressing instant ideas and following the actions with **spontaneous reactions** allows **freedom of thought and builds confidence** through inclusion and acceptance. The members' ideas should, hopefully, be of a developed standard and natural cohesion and fluidity should be witnessed.)*

Total time: 45 mins

Warm Up: **Shake Hands Intro**   **5 mins**

Instructions: Ask the group to think of one positive thing about themselves and one personal dislike. Example: Jess likes her long hair and intends to grow it even longer. However, she does not like cabbage and refuses to eat it. Ask each member to move about the space to greet another member by shaking their hand and exchanging their likes and dislikes. Repeat this five times. Ask the group to remember who they have visited as next week they will complete the task again but meet up with different people.

*(Purpose of game: This game helps with **personal disclosure and self-evaluation**. To acknowledge and accept positive and negative things about yourself can help structure a balanced individual. Some people find it **hard to accept praise, and others criticism**, and talking about yourself can sometimes prove to be difficult or embarrassing **if you lack self-esteem**. So having the chance to talk to others you have built a working and trusting relationship with may help those with disclosure issues.)*

Game 1: **Sabotage**    **10 mins**

Instructions: Ask the members to get into a group of three and explain that two of the members are to start a conversation. The third member is to subtly sabotage the conversation. Example: Member 1 says 'Hi Brandon, how well did you do in your spelling test?' Member 2 replies 'Not so good, I had hoped...' Member 3 suddenly starts a sneezing fit and interrupts the flow of speech. They apologise and the conversation continues until Member 3 interrupts again with another sneezing fit...etc. Let each member have the chance to sabotage a conversation and encourage them to try innovative and inventive ways to do this.

Examples:

   asking for directions to somewhere
   coughing fit
   making a telephone call
   fidgeting.

*(Purpose of game: This game allows the members to explore different distraction techniques and explore the **manipulation of language**. It is a fun way to be **inventive** and introduces the **skill of comedy** in performance.)*

Drama Sessions for Primary Schools and Drama Clubs

Exercise 1: **Time Machine – The Past** **30 mins**

Instructions: Explain that the group will take part in a group improvisation. The teacher becomes the narrator and guides the action along to make a group performance. Line the group up at one side of the room and explain that a time machine is stored underneath the floorboards and when it is called up it will take the group on a journey. Ask the members to hold their arms out in front of them and wiggle their fingers whilst humming. Explain that as the humming gets louder the time machine will break through the floorboards and stand before them ready for action. The teacher claps their hands and explains the time machine is ready, but first they must line up to enter the pod. Explain that before them is a door, and select one member to enter the key code for the door to open. Then ask the group to enter the machine one by one and look for their seat as it has their name on it. As they mime entry, guide them into a sitting circle. Once everyone is sitting down explain that a computer screen is in front of them and the armrests have a number and letter keypad for them to type in the necessary data. Also explain that there is a seatbelt [mime action] and safety helmet [mime action] to put on. Ask the group to decide where in history they would like to visit. Example: dinosaurs/Egypt/western America. Then ask them to type on their keypad the following data: location and date. Then ask them to turn three knobs, flick three switches, lift up a lever and press the big green launch button in front of them. Act out a seated motion of travel. Example: Jiggle about on bottoms as if moving through space then crescendo with a group clap. The teacher asks a member to look out of the window behind them and to describe what they see. Go with that vision. Explain that they have travelled to this destination on a mission. They are to find an item to take back to school for further experiments. Example: dinosaur egg/Egyptian sovereign/western sheriff badge. Send out each member from the time machine explaining that once they have their item they must come straight back ready for departure. Let the members act their individual exploration plays without guidance. After a short time ask everyone to come back to the time machine for departure. Go through the same routine of putting on seatbelts, helmets and typing in destination data. Turn the knobs, flick the switches, lift the lever and press the green button to travel back home. Once landed, ask the group to leave the time machine and to take their item with them. If there is time, reset the time machine back under the floorboards for another adventure next week.

*(Purpose of exercise: This exercise is all about the art of storytelling and the **development of the imagination**. Listening and being guided through the magical experience enthrals the group. Then being able **to express and explore their individual ideas**, focuses the ability to role play and indulge in their personal ideas and fantasy.)*

Total time: 45 mins

Warm Up: **Shake Hands Intro – Repeat**   **5 mins**

Instructions: Ask the group to think of a different positive thing and one personal dislike about themselves to that of last session. Example: Dean is proud of his achievements in football and believes he is top scorer this season. However, he does not like his training programme and is quite lazy. Ask each member to find a partner and ask them to greet another member by shaking their hand and exchanging their likes and dislikes. Repeat this five times. Ask the group to remember who they have visited as next week they will complete the task again with the aim of meeting up with different people.

*(Purpose of game: Repeating this game helps develop a deeper understanding of **personal disclosure and self-evaluation**. To acknowledge and accept positive and negative aspects about yourself can help structure a balanced individual. Some people find it **hard to accept praise, and others criticism**, and talking about yourself can sometimes prove to be difficult or embarrassing **if you lack self-esteem**. So having the chance to talk to others you have built a working and trusting relationship with may help those with disclosure issues.)*

Game 1: **Don't Make Me Laugh!**   **10 mins**

Instructions: Ask the group to get into pairs and explain that one member is to remain focused and straight-faced whilst the other member attempts to make them laugh. The member trying to make their partner laugh can try different styles and techniques. Example: telling jokes, pulling faces or tickling. The object of the game is to not under any circumstances break the focus and give in to laughter. Swap roles and repeat.

*(Purpose of game: This is a fun game that introduces the performance skill of **remaining focused under difficult circumstances**. It shows the members that concentration can be sustained even under extreme circumstances and this in turn helps them to acknowledge their **personal inner strength**.)*

Exercise 1: **Time Machine – The Future**   **30 mins**

Instructions: Explain that the group will take part in another group improvisation. The teacher becomes the narrator and guides the action along to make a group performance. Line the group up at one side of the room and explain that the time machine is stored underneath the floorboards and when it is called up it will take the group on a journey. Ask the members to hold their arms out in front of them and wiggle their fingers whilst humming. Explain that as the humming gets louder the time machine will break through the floorboards and stand before them ready for action. The teacher claps their hands and explains that the time machine is ready, but first they must line up to enter the pod.

Explain that before them is a door, and select one member to enter the key code for the door to open. Then ask the group to enter the machine one by one and look for their seat as it has their name on it. As they mime entry, guide them into a sitting circle. Once everyone is sitting down explain that a computer screen is in front of them and the armrests have a number and letter keypad for you to type in the necessary data. Also explain that there is a seatbelt [mime action] and safety helmet [mime action] to put on. Ask the group to decide where in the future they would like to visit. Example: planet Mars/City of London/their school. Then ask them to type into their keypad the following data: location and date. Then ask them to turn three knobs, flick three switches, lift up a lever and press the big green launch button in front of them. Act out a seated motion of travel. Example: Jiggle about on bottoms as if moving through space then crescendo with a group clap. The teacher asks a member to look out of the window behind them and to describe what they see. Go with that vision. Explain that they have travelled to this destination on a mission. They are to find an item to take back in time to conduct some experiments. Example: alien food/souvenir of London/futuristic school book. Send out each member from the time machine explaining that once they have their item they must come straight back ready for departure. Let the members act their individual plays without guidance. After a short time ask everyone to come back to the time machine for departure. Go through the same routine of putting on seatbelts, helmets and typing in destination data. Turn the knobs, flick the switches, lift the lever and press the green button to travel back home. Once landed, ask the group to leave the time machine and to take their item with them. If there is time, reset the time machine back under the floorboards.

*(Purpose of exercise: Repeating this exercise allows the members another chance to explore the art of storytelling and the **development of the imagination**. Again, listening and being guided through the magical experience enthrals the group and enables them **to express and explore their individual ideas** through role play, and indulges them in personal ideas and fantasy.)*

Total time: 45 mins

Warm Up: **Shake Hands Intro – Repeat**   **5 mins**

Instructions: Ask the group to think of another positive thing and another personal dislike about themselves different to the previous session. Example: Sarah is proud of the fact that she won an award for her drawing as it took two days to complete. However, she is disgruntled by the fact that she has to put more effort into her spellings because she doesn't always get them right. Ask each member to greet another member by shaking hands and exchanging their likes and dislikes. Repeat this five times. Ask the group to remember who they have visited today as eventually you are aiming to meet everyone in the whole group.

*(Purpose of game: Repeating this game helps develop a deeper understanding of **personal disclosure and self-evaluation**. To acknowledge and accept positive and negative aspects about yourself can help structure a balanced individual. Some people find it **hard to accept praise, and others criticism**, and talking about yourself can sometimes prove to be difficult or embarrassing **if you lack self-esteem**. So having another chance to talk to others you have built a working and trusting relationship which may help tackle further disclosure issues.)*

Game 1: **The Next Word Is…**   **10 mins**

Instructions: Ask the group to sit in a circle and explain that the group will make up a story, sentence by sentence, with one simple rule that the last word in the previous sentence must start the next one. Example: Member 1 says 'Once upon a time there was a toy doll.' Member 2 says 'Doll wasn't feeling too well and decided to call for a doctor.' Member 3 says 'Doctor Smith came around to visit doll straight away'…etc. Ask every member in the circle to contribute a sentence until the story is complete.

*(Purpose of game: This game uses a fun approach to show members how the English language can be used to produce a **colourful and unpredictable story line**. It takes great thought and concentration to **build a working story line** and it sometimes can prove to be quite challenging.)*

Exercise 1: **Aeroplane Impro**   **30 mins**

Instructions: Select two members to be aeroplane pilots and place two chairs at one end of the space for them to sit on. Then select two members to be cabin crew and to stand by the chairs. Then select one member to be at passport control and place them in the middle of the space. Cast another member to be at an airport check-in desk and place them at the opposite side of the space to the pilots. Explain to the rest of the group that they will be passengers on an

Drama Sessions for Primary Schools and Drama Clubs

aeroplane that is about to take off. Ask them to line up in pairs to check in their luggage at the desk. Once they have checked in their luggage they are to move on to passport control and mime showing their passports to the controller. Once past the controller, they are greeted by the cabin crew and shown to their seats where they sit down on the floor in pairs and wait for the rest of the passengers to join them. Once everyone is seated, ask the pilots to introduce themselves and explain that they are about to fly to a hot destination. Then guide the cabin crew through the flight safety brief and ask them to check that all the seatbelts are fastened. Then instruct the pilot to count down from ten to take off. Mime being airborne with the crew walking up and down the aisle offering drinks and snacks. Suddenly the aeroplane flies into turbulence; instruct the pilots to ask everyone to be seated. Suddenly one engine fails; ask the pilots to make an emergency landing. The aeroplane crash-lands onto a desert island but luckily no one is badly hurt. Ask everyone to get out of the aeroplane and hunt for some food and return to the camp with their findings. Decide that they must have a shelter so they can sleep under cover, then send everyone out to find wood etc. to make it. Ask them to make campfires and SOS signs in the sand and then decide that they must all eat and sit around the campfire to cook what they had previously found. Then ask the group to go to sleep in their shelters. When sleeping, they hear the sound of a rescue helicopter, they all jump up and wave arms in the air to attract attention. Select two members to be the helicopter pilots, and one by one the members mime climbing up a rope ladder to safety. Once all members are safe the improvisation is concluded.

*(Purpose of exercise: This exercise is all about the art of storytelling and the **development of the imagination through role play**. Listening and being guided through the magical experience encourages the group to **self-express** and demonstrates how creative ideas can be placed into a tangible performance.)*

Total time: 45 mins

Session materials: cloak (or similar, i.e. blanket)

Warm Up: **Shake Hands Intro – Repeat**　　　　　　**5 mins**

Instructions: Ask the group to think of another positive thing and another personal dislike about themselves different to the previous session. Example: Tim thinks his reading skills are good but wishes he could grow a bit taller as he is the smallest in his group of friends. Ask each member to greet another member by shaking hands and exchanging their likes and dislikes. Repeat this five times. Ask the group to remember who they have visited today as they should now know something personal about nearly every member of the group.

*(Purpose of game: Repeating this game helps develop a deeper understanding of **personal disclosure and self-evaluation**. To acknowledge and accept positive and negative aspects about yourself can help structure a balanced individual. Some people find it **hard to accept praise, and others criticism**, and talking about yourself can sometimes prove to be difficult or embarrassing **if you lack self-esteem**. So having another chance to talk to others you have built a working and trusting relationship which may help tackle further disclosure issues.)*

Game 1: **Witches and Wizards**　　　　　　　　**10 mins**

Instructions: One member is chosen to be a witch/wizard, wraps the cloak around their shoulders and hides in the corner of the room. The group are to move casually about the space playing as if in the playground. Suddenly the witch/wizard appears and all the children curl up into tight balls hiding their faces. The witch/wizard selects one member, covers them with the cloak and holds them captive. The rest of the group stand up and look around to see who is missing. Once they realise, they call out: 'Release [name]' three times. The witch/wizard will only release the captive child if the group performs a task for them. Example: Witch says: 'Only if you hop on one leg for a count of 20' etc. When completed, the captured child is released and becomes the next witch/wizard.

*(Purpose of game: This game further develops the sensory skill and explores a **simple form of problem-solving**. Being made aware of **subtle changes** within their environment **promotes independent thinking** by analysing a pattern of change and making constructive conclusions.)*

Drama Sessions for Primary Schools and Drama Clubs

Exercise 1: **Submarine Improvisation**  **30 mins**

Instructions: Explain that the members are a group of trained scuba divers on a mission to the bottom of the sea. Select one member to be the submarine pilot and ask them to sit at one end of the room. Everyone else is to mime changing into a wetsuit and swimming one by one into the submarine by sitting in an oval shape on the floor. Once in the submarine, ask the group to check that they have all the necessary equipment to complete the mission. Ask the pilot to start lowering the submarine to the bottom of the sea. As the pilot is doing this, ask the group members to mime putting on their flippers, air tank, goggles and mouthpiece. The pilot then calls out that the submarine has reached its designated spot and divers can be released. The pilot then opens the special hatch that allows each member to exit the submarine one by one and explore the bottom of the sea. Then choose half of the group to become mermaids/mermen and ask them to act out the actions etc. whilst the remaining divers swim and observe. Then swap roles, ask the divers to be sea urchins and ask the other half to swim and observe as divers once again. Swap once again and ask the divers to be sharks whilst the other half of the group swims for safety. Then ask all the members to be divers again searching for the pirates' treasure at the bottom of the sea. Let the members improvise short plays of hunting and finding the treasure. Once the divers have the treasure, one by one they re-enter the submarine for departure. The pilot takes their position once more as the divers remove their equipment, clean it and store it away. The submarine arrives at the surface, and one by one the group swim to shore. Once everyone is on the shore the improvisation is complete.

*(Purpose of exercise: Again, this exercise is all about the art of storytelling and the **development of the imagination through role play**. Listening and being guided through the magical experience gives further confidence in **self-expression** and demonstrates how creative ideas can be placed into tangible performances.)*

Total time: 45 mins

Warm Up: **Shake Hands Intro – Repeat**   **5 mins**

Instructions: Ask the group to think of another positive thing and another personal dislike about themselves different to the previous sessions. Example: Chloe is proud of the fact she is in the top set for brass band as she enjoys playing the trumpet. However, she does not like outdoor PE during the winter as she hates the cold. Ask each member to greet another member by shaking hands and exchanging their likes and dislikes. Repeat this five times. Ask the group to remember who they have visited today as they should now know something personal about nearly every member of the group.

*(Purpose of game: Repeating this game for a final time and having spoken with most members on a deep and personal level you should now have **created a feeling of equilibrium within the group** and a deeper understanding of **personal disclosure and self-evaluation**. Acknowledging praise and constructive criticism is a life skill developed only through experience and this exercise helps introduce this.)*

Game 1: **Random Counting – Repeat**    **5 mins**

Instructions: Ask the group to sit in a circle and then to face out into the space (not face into the circle as usual). With their backs to each other, the teacher explains that the group will attempt to count to 20 spontaneously and at random. Example: One member starts by calling out number 1. Then a different member calls out number 2. A third member then calls out number 3 . . . etc. It is never discussed or pre-planned as to who will call out the next number. Once a member has called out a number they are not to call out again. If two people shout out at the same time, the group has to start the counting all over again. The members will now note their best-ever score.

*(Purpose of game: Repeating this game for the final time allows the group to feel the **team cohesion and support they have accomplished** over the three terms of drama classes.)*

Exercise 1: **The Circus**   **35 mins**

Instructions: Put the group into five smaller groups (see Glossary, Smaller-sized groups) and give each group an act from the circus. Example: 1. unicyclists. 2. lion tamers. 3. elephant parade with trainers. 4. clowns. 5. trapeze artists. Then ask the small groups to find a space within the room and devise a short performance to show to a circus audience. This should take no longer than ten minutes. Once everyone has completed and rehearsed their short play the teacher asks the whole group to sit in an audience position. Then select one member from the group to be the circus ringmaster who, with help from the teacher, will invite each act, one by one, to perform in the circus tent. The ringmaster starts the show by welcoming everybody and then calling up the first act to start. When the short play has been performed, the audience members join the smaller group in the performance area and join in that circus act. Example: Everyone becomes the unicyclists and pretends to cycle around the space ... etc. Each performance ends with loud cheers and applause and the ringmaster introduces the next act. Once everyone has performed their short play, ask the group to line up and take a group bow.

*(Purpose of exercise: This task helps bring together most elements that have been introduced over the past three terms. It creates a **devised performance** (short, planned plays) mixed with exploring the **improvised performance** (making it up on the spot as a whole group). It **builds confidence** through the art of **performing to others** and helps **stimulate creativity** through fantasy role play. It explores **working relationships in teams** (the devising of the mini play) as well as experimenting with time-related tasks. Bringing this all together with all the other aspects of social and behavioural skills should produce rounded and progressive individuals.)*

Total time: 45 mins

Parental session

Warm Up: **Name Game**   **5 mins**

Instructions: With the group in a circle facing one another, each member takes a turn to introduce themselves with a movement/action to their name, then the rest of the group copy the action exactly. Example: Alison does a star jump and shouts her name at the same time. The group then copies.

*(Purpose of game: This game allows the child to express themselves as an individual. It looks at **multi-task collaboration**; to move; to speak; to think; all at the same time. This game quickly displays those **with little confidence** and those who will need extra encouragement.)*

Game 1: **Gibberish with Translator**   **10 mins**

Instructions: Sitting in a circle, ask three members to stand up to play. Explain that two members are to talk gibberish (a language of noises and sounds) to each other with animated actions whilst the third member translates the conversation into English for the rest of the group. Of course, there is no planning and the translator just explains what they believe the conversation is about. The group takes turns to play until all have contributed.

*(Purpose of game: This game is just a further introduction to **breaking inhibitions and building confidence**. Having the added element of translator allows the body language displayed by the talking members to be analysed and interpreted. By doing this we show the watching members that we often **provide non-verbal communication through involuntary and voluntary body movement/language**.)*

Exercise 1: **Time Machine – The Past**   **30 mins**

Instructions: Explain that the group will take part in a group improvisation. The teacher becomes the narrator and guides the action along to make a group performance. Line the group up at one side of the room and explain that a time machine is stored underneath the floorboards and when it is called up it will take the group on a journey. Ask the members to hold their arms out in front of them and wiggle their fingers whilst humming. Explain that as the humming gets louder the time machine will break through the floorboards and stand before them ready for action. The teacher claps their hands and explains the time machine is ready, but first they must line up to enter the pod. Explain that before them is a door and select one member to enter the key code for the door to open. Then ask the group to enter the machine one by one and look for their seat as it has their name on it. As they mime entry, guide them into a sitting circle. Once everyone is sitting down explain that a computer screen is in front of them and the armrests have a number and letter keypad for them to type in the necessary data. Also explain that there is a seatbelt [mime action] and safety helmet [mime action] to put on. Ask the group to decide where in history they would like to visit. Example: dinosaurs/Egypt/western America. Then ask them to type on their keypad the following data: location and date. Then ask them to turn three knobs, flick three switches, lift up a lever and press the big green launch button in front of them. Act out a seated motion of travel. Example: Jiggle about on bottoms as if moving through space then crescendo with a group clap. The teacher asks a member to look out of the window behind them and to describe what they see. Go with that vision. Explain that they have travelled to this destination on a mission. They are to find an item to take back to school for further experiments. Example: dinosaur egg/Egyptian sovereign/western sheriff badge. Send out each member from the time machine explaining that once they have their item they must come straight back ready for departure. Let the members act their individual exploration plays without guidance. After a short time ask everyone to come back to the time machine for departure. Go through the same routine of putting on seatbelts, helmets and typing in destination data. Turn the knobs, flick the switches, lift the lever and press the green button to travel back home. Once landed, ask the group to leave the time machine and to take their item with them. If there is time, reset the time machine back under the floorboards for another adventure next week.

*(Purpose of exercise: This exercise is all about the art of storytelling and the **development of the imagination**. Listening and being guided through the magical experience enthrals the group. Then being able **to express and explore their individual ideas**, focuses the ability to role play and indulge in their personal ideas and fantasy.)*

Total time: 45 mins

Parental session: notes

Welcome to our drama session. I thought it would be useful to provide you with a brief outline of the exercises we will be doing today, so that you can have a better understanding of our aims and achievements.

Warm Up: **Name Game**

This exercise allows the child to express themselves as an individual. It also looks at multi-task collaboration; to move; to speak; to think; all at the same time.

Game 1: **Gibberish with Translator**

This game is about breaking inhibitions and building confidence. Having the added support of a translator allows the body language of the talking members to be studied and interpreted. By playing this game, we show the watching members that we can often read non-verbal communication (body language/movement) and gauge information from that.

Exercise 1: **Time Machine**

This exercise is all about the art of storytelling and the development of the imagination. Listening and being guided through the magical experience captivates the group. Then, being able to express and explore their own individual ideas focuses the ability to role play and indulges in their personal dramatic fantasy.

Drama Sessions for Primary Schools and Drama Clubs

CHAPTER 5

Smaller space relocation session plans

Smaller space relocation

Warm Up: **Name Game** 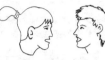 **5 mins**

Instructions: With the group standing in a circle facing one another, each member takes a turn to introduce themselves with a movement/action to their name, then the rest of the group copy the action exactly. **When located in a smaller room, ask the group to consider movements of height and levels. Example: reaching up with a long stretch. As an alternative, ask them to sit on the floor with legs out in front of them and create movements that are much smaller and precise. Example: wiggling toes, clicking fingers in conjunction with their name etc.**

*(Purpose of game: This game allows the child to express themselves as an individual. It looks at **multi-task collaboration**; to move; to speak; to think; all at the same time. This game quickly displays those **with little confidence** and those who will need extra encouragement.)*

Game 1: **Random Counting**  **5 mins**

Instructions: Ask the group to sit in a circle and then to face out into the space (not face into the circle as usual). With their backs to each other the teacher explains that the group will attempt to count to 20 spontaneously and at random. Example: One member starts by calling out number 1. Then a different member calls out number 2. A third member then calls out number 3 . . . etc. It is never discussed or pre-planned as to who will call out the next number. Once a member has called out a number they are not to call out again. If two people shout out at the same time, the group has to start the counting all over again. Note the highest number achieved for future reference.

*(Purpose of exercise: This game creates **team cohesion** and working together to achieve an end goal. It helps show the group how much of a united front they can be and how listening and perceiving others' actions can help them to make useful judgements. It will also show some members how easily they can become frustrated as unsuccessful attempts will trigger certain members' disappointment.)*

Exercise 1: **The Next Word Is . . .**  **10 mins**

Instructions: Ask the group to sit in a circle and explain that the group will make up a story, sentence by sentence, with one simple rule that the last word in the previous sentence must start the next one. Example: Member 1 says 'Once upon a time there was a toy doll'. Member 2 says 'Doll wasn't feeling too well and decided to call for a doctor'. Member 3 says 'Doctor Smith came around to visit doll straightaway' . . . etc. Ask every member in the circle to contribute a sentence until the story is complete.

*(Purpose of game: This game uses a fun approach to show members how the English language can be used to produce a **colourful and unpredictable story line**. It takes great thought and concentration to **build a working story line** and can sometimes prove to be quite challenging.)*

Exercise 1: **Adam and Eve**   **25 mins**

Instructions: Ask the group to create a rectangle (rather than a circle) and ask them to sit with their legs crossed and arms out with palms facing forward to create a barrier of protection. Then select two members to be blindfolded and place them in the middle of the rectangle. The two members are only allowed to move around the rectangle on their hands and knees. One member is called Adam and they are to try to catch the other member called Eve. Eve is to try to escape the touch of Adam. The game begins with Adam and Eve at opposite ends of the rectangle with the remaining group members being silent and protecting Adam and Eve from heading out of the rectangle by gently guiding them back inwards with their hands.

*(Purpose of exercise: This exercise again looks at **sensory skills and the use of heightening senses** by taking one away. It also looks at listening skills and the recognition of perceiving someone is close by. **Team spirit** is built by looking after and supporting the members conducting the exercise. It provides great **enjoyment through observing others** and making judgements from what they see before them.)*

Total time: 45 mins

Warm Up: **Name Game**   **5 mins**

Instructions: With the group standing in a circle facing one another, each member takes a turn to introduce themselves with a movement/action to their name, then the rest of the group copy the action exactly. **When located in a smaller room, ask the group to consider movements of height and levels. Example: reaching up with a long stretch. As an alternative, ask them to sit on the floor with legs out in front of them and create movements that are much smaller and precise. Example: wiggling toes, clicking fingers in conjunction with their name etc.**

(Purpose of game: This game allows the child to express themselves as an individual. It looks at **multi-task collaboration***; to move; to speak; to think; all at the same time. This game quickly displays those* **with little confidence** *and those who will need extra encouragement.)*

Game 1: **The Plasticine Pass**   **10 mins**

Instructions: With the group sitting in a circle, take an imaginary lump of plasticine and roll it into an object of use. Example: toothbrush, hairbrush. Perform a mime action so members can guess the object. Then pass the object to the person to the right where they use it for a short time and then squash it to make their new object. Continue around the circle until the end.

(Purpose of game: This simple game starts to build improvisation skills with **independent thinking and expression***. It allows you to give* **one-to-one encouragement** *to every pupil in a focused setting. It allows personal praise and acknowledgement, and this, in turn, builds confidence.)*

Exercise 1: **Bang!**   **15 mins**

Instructions: Standing in a circle, explain that you are all cowboys and cowgirls with two pistols in your holster. The teacher starts the game by calling a member's name. That person then ducks to the floor and the two people either side have a shoot-out by pointing their fingers at each other and shouting 'bang'. The first person to say the word bang is the winner, and the loser sits down in their circle placement. If, however, the person whose name is called does not duck down quickly enough, they are out, as they get hit by the bullets from the shoot-out. When only two people are left standing they step into the middle of the circle and place themselves back-to-back as if in a 'showdown'. They step three steps away from each other and listen for a selected member of the sitting crowd to shout the word bang, on which they turn and shoot each other by shouting the word bang. The ultimate winner is the person who shouts 'bang' first.

*(Purpose of game: This game is all about **focus**. The group has to remain focused throughout the whole exercise in order to prevent losing. The game changes each time a player sits out, so it is about **processing the ever-changing information correctly** and adapting your actions accordingly. It also allows self-expression, as it produces an authorised emotional outlet in a controlled context.)*

Exercise 2: **The Bomb Shelter**  **15 mins**

Instructions: Select five members to stand in front of the group and ask them to each think of a famous person they can impersonate. Explain that they are in World War II and they have all been placed in a bomb shelter for their safety. However, there is only enough equipment and food to help save four lives and one of them will have to leave and fend for themselves in the war zone alone. Each member is to devise a short speech on why they should be allowed to stay and how crucial it is that they survive. Example: The Queen; if she were to die, who would make the decisions that governed the Kingdom? Once everyone has spoken, the group decides who should stay and who should be evicted by clapping. The one with the loudest clapping should be the one that leaves. They act a mini mime of opening the bomb shelter door and evicting them into the war zone. Repeat.

*(Purpose of exercise: This exercise is all about **learning negotiation skills**. It looks at how to build a constructive argument and **how to put across a definitive point of view**. It is all about verbal communication and how to learn to **express their ideas and opinions** in a constructive manner. The acting is just the fun tool that allows this exercise to exist.)*

Total time: 45 mins

Warm Up: **Name Game**   **5 mins**

Instructions: With the group standing in a circle facing one another, each member takes a turn to introduce themselves with a movement/action to their name, then the rest of the group copy the action exactly. **When located in a smaller room, ask the group to consider movements of height and levels. Example: reaching up with a long stretch. As an alternative, ask them to sit on the floor with legs out in front of them and create movements that are much smaller and precise. Example: wiggling toes, clicking fingers in conjunction with their name etc.**

*(Purpose of game: This game allows the child to express themselves as an individual. It looks at **multi-task collaboration**; to move; to speak; to think; all at the same time. This game quickly displays those **with little confidence** and those who will need extra encouragement.)*

Game 1: **Zip, Zap, Bong!**   **10 mins**

Instructions: With the group in a standing circle explain that the members are all very important transmitters in a power circuit. The electricity can only be transported to one another in the following ways. You can pass the electricity to the people either side of you by placing your hands palm to palm and pointing to them and saying 'zip'. You can only pass the electricity across the circle by placing your hands palm to palm and throwing the ball of power across to an individual and saying 'zap'. You can choose to reject the power being sent to you by doing a star jump and saying 'bong' in the direction it came from. This sends the power back to that person. Members get frazzled by the extreme heat of the electricity if they hold on to it for too long or say the wrong word to the action. Once someone is out, the teacher continues the game by doing the first action. The winner is the last member standing.

*(Purpose of exercise: This game is all about improving **concentration and focus**. The game is fast and unpredictable and this challenges its members into **thinking ahead with quick but calculated reactions**. It teaches responsibility as their attention and focus on the forever-evolving action is the only way they can stay in the game.)*

Game 1: **Feeling Game**   **10 mins**

Instructions: The group forms a circle and one member is chosen to be blindfolded. This person is then gently spun around and then let loose to walk into a standing member. The blindfolded person then feels the face of that member to guess who they are. If they guess correctly it is that member's turn to be blindfolded. If they guess incorrectly they are to move on to another person to guess again.

Drama Sessions for Primary Schools and Drama Clubs

*(Purpose of game: This game attempts to **break inhibitions** by allowing the embarrassment of touch to be explored through a fun game. It also **enhances sensory recognition** and the development of **recall memory** through game play.)*

Exercise 1: **The Photo Game** 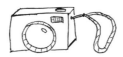 **20 mins**

Instructions: With the group in an audience position the teacher explains that they have brought along their imaginary photo album and there are photos of the group inside. Mime getting a particular photo out and show the members, explaining that this photo is of them on the beach. One by one, ask the members to join the acting space in a frozen mime position. Example: sunbathing, building sandcastles, surfing, swimming etc. When half of the group are placed in the photo, the photo is finished. The teacher then calls 'action/freeze' to members, one by one, and they show a mini play (improvisation) to the remaining audience members. Example: the sunbathers apply lotion. The sandcastle is destroyed. The surfer falls off their board. The swimmer starts to drown. Once everyone in the photo has performed individually the whole photo comes to life and a play (improvisation) ensues. The teacher calls a timely 'freeze' and explains the frozen image now in front of them is the photograph previously shown. Repeat.

Photos: **hospital   wedding   theme park   circus   hairdressers**

*(Purpose of exercise: This exercise builds imagination and **storytelling skills**. Showing individual ideas in an improvised context allows a member to **freely express themselves**. It helps build confidence through performing their ideas to others and being actively praised for their personal efforts.)*

Total time: 45 mins

Risk assessment form

Risk Assessment – Drama Vision – After-school Drama Clubs

	Week 1	Week 2	Week 3	Week 4	Week 5
Fire doors have free access					
Fire extinguisher is in place					
External doors are secure					
Corridor doors are closed					
Gym apparatus put away and secured					
All electrical apparatus secured					
No spillages or the like					
Other: please give details					

Drama Sessions for Primary Schools and Drama Clubs

Week 6	Week 7	Week 8	Week 9	Week 10	Week 11

Appendix: Risk assessment form

Glossary

Below is a list of words and dramatic terms explained in further detail for your reference.

Audience position: This describes the placement of the watching members. It usually means a traditional proscenium position (see below) where the watching members sit directly in front of the performance.

Smaller-sized groups: When asked to place the large class into smaller groups you have three options:

1. Ask the group to **assemble themselves** into smaller set groups independently. This is good for timekeeping as it happens quickly; however, friends will work with friends and this can be a misdemeanour, as they tend to be distracted easily and do not always work to their best capability. Also it doesn't encourage inclusion or unison as they aren't working with different members of the group or out of their comfort zone.
2. **Mark the set number** from the sitting positions in the circle. Example: Count around the circle setting groups of say five. This method does mix people together but the large majority will still be working with friends as they tend to sit together in clusters. Also you have to be careful that selected segregation doesn't occur as this can actually create alienation and cause unnecessary friction in the working relationship.
3. **Random counting.** Nominate (say 5) members to different parts of the room with a number between 1 and 5. Then count around the circle providing each sitting member with a number between 1 and 5 succinctly. That member then joins the relevant allocated team. This is the best format to achieve random groupings and builds better results as well as helps build group union.

Devise: This means to build and create a performance from an initial source; to make up a play that is to be rehearsed before it is performed.

Improvised/improvisation: To produce ideas and creative output that has not been previously rehearsed/discussed/planned. It is to be spontaneous, on-the-spot movement/dialogue.

The round: Describes the positioning of the audience when watching the performed action. It details the audience encompassing the action and watching from all possible angles. Usually this is done by setting the performance inside a circle.

The arena: Describes the audience in a tiered seating arrangement and can also encompass the action similar to the round (as in Roman arenas). The best way to achieve this arrangement is by setting different levels for the audience to observe the action. This can be done by having one line of members lying down on their fronts; then a second line of kneeling members and a third line of standing members. This can create a tiered-like feeling for both audience and performers.

The proscenium: Describes a traditional audience position where the action is set in front of the seated audience. The audience is classed as the 'fourth wall' to the three-sided stage.